Japanese Home Cooking

Simple Recipes for Healthy Living!

Reiko Suenaga

Photographer
Sadamu Saito

Published by special arrangement with TranNet KK, Tokyo, Japan

Veronica Lane Books
www.veronicalanebooks.com
email:etan@veronicalanebooks.com
2554 Lincoln Blvd. Ste 142, Los Angeles, CA 90291 USA
Tel/Fax: +1 (800) 651-1001 / Intl: +1 (310) 745-0162

ISBN: 978-0-9826513-9-1

Library of Congress Cataloging-In-Publication Data

161 p. cm

Summary:Simple Japanese home cooking recipes with related Japanese traditional
and modern food culture information are presented.

Dedicated to loving memory of my late mother. ✿

Table of Contents

Foreword

I was very fortunate to have the chance to stay with my family in Australia and Mexico for several years because of my husband's work. I had extraordinary food experiences, particularly in Mexico. While there I lived on the premises of an international organization. I enjoyed the international atmosphere every day, and I felt especially lucky to be able to savor home cooking from all over the world. This environment gave me a great opportunity to try very different tastes, ingredients and eating practices that I would have never known if I had stayed in Japan. It was this tasty experience that later made me think about food culture in Japan, which eventually led to this book.

All of the home cooking I had then was wonderful and delicious, no matter what country it came from. It made me realize that there is no home cooking that tastes bad. After a while, however, a strange feeling occurred to me. After eating such cooking so often, I began to feel like something was missing – the wonderful home cooking that I was raised on. Even after I had stuffed myself with delicious food, I felt somehow restless and could not feel completely satisfied. Soon I could not help eating even a tiny bit of Japanese food to end the day's meal. I had little idea why I was like that at that time and did not really think about it. But years later, words from my daughter, who had just started studying abroad, reminded me of that unanswered question. I was on the phone talking with her, and she unintentionally said "I really miss your cooking." It hit me as a surprise and made me think: what does that really mean?

Among people all over the world, Japanese people are the least able to verbally express their love for someone. Whenever I see Westerners say "I love you" to their family members and hug each other, I say to myself, "I could never do that." On the other hand, I know it is impossible to communicate with others without expressing our feelings. Then how have Japanese people shown their feelings to others all those years? I thought about it. We Japanese probably have other ways of saying "I love you." I realized that one of them must be cooking and eating together, which happens every day. Traditionally, Japanese mothers used to have taken care of almost all the work concerning home. Despite their busy schedules, they

spend an incredible amount of time preparing good meals for their families. When going out for an event or something, they make beautiful and nutritious lunch boxes or *onigiri* (rice balls) for them. *Onigiri* is a very simple recipe, but mothers make them as if they were putting their love into each grain of rice. That kind of love surely gets across to their family members. Even if there is not a phrase "I love you," *onigiri* itself represent the mothers' love for their families. They do not have to say "I love you" verbally. To Japanese people, the taste of mothers' cooking is the taste of mothers' love, and that is also the taste of heartwarming home. To Japanese, cooking and eating are not just habits through which people get necessary nutrition, but also a returning home – the place where mothers are.

The action of cooking and processing ingredients and enjoying tasting various flavors with the food is not seen in other animals. This is a culture exclusive to us humans. Children eat meals prepared by their mothers and fathers. They grow by doing so countless times and without realizing it, they've absorbed and learned a food culture that is unique to each family. Because of this food culture that is handed down from parents to children, people are able to "return home" through the practice of cooking and eating even when they grow up and are away from home. The food culture that children experience becomes the foundation for their eating and dietary habits. In the good old days, Japanese mothers knew only too well that cooking and eating together had the power to nurture young ones' hearts and minds. Back then, mothers hardly asked for recognition, but they were unarguably the key presence in each family, always giving love to their families, keeping a strong tie among family members, and protecting and nurturing the most important unit, the family, upon which every society is built, through preparing meals and eating them together. Mothers taught food culture to children. Mothers themselves were home for children to come back to.

In modern Japan and other developed countries, people can easily get delicious foods ready to serve right away. I am sure that they are nutritious and taste wonderful. However, suppose that you keep eating such ready-made foods every day, do you think that you will be really satisfied? Don't you think that you may feel like something is missing? If so, that may be the same something that I felt was missing when I could not be satisfied by eating foods in foreign countries, however delicious they were, or that my daughter was requesting as a mother's taste on the phone. What I might have been looking for at that time may have been the taste of my original food culture – "home" to be more exact. I am sure that my daughter did not mean all that when she said, "I really miss your cooking." But her words made me realize all of this.

The dishes introduced in this book are very common in households all over Japan. However, if you were to try to make traditional Japanese recipes outside of Japan, you would find that it is quite difficult to obtain all the necessary ingredients. So I chose very commonly prepared Japanese meals and converted the recipes using ingredients that are readily available all over the world. I hope that Japanese living overseas will be able to "return home" and enjoy "mother's cooking" more easily with these recipes. In addition, I will be very pleased if this book is helpful to people in other countries who are interested in Japanese cooking and food culture.

Introduction

"We went to a Japanese restaurant yesterday and today we feel so healthy," an American friend of mine happily told me one day. Of course, she was joking, but her words somehow lingered in my ears.

Japanese food has gained so much in popularity worldwide that it is now no longer seen as an uncommon cuisine to enjoy at a Japanese restaurant or *sushi* bar in any major city. Many books about Japanese food and cooking have been also published with more and more people showing widespread interest in it. But what has caused this worldwide fascination with the Japanese diet?

For one, many people were attracted to the exotic tastes that they had never experienced before. Japanese-style cooking uses ingredients that many would never have imagined eating, and produces unusual flavors through using simple combinations of different seasonings. This way of cooking gave those people a totally new perspective on ingredients and led them to discover a whole range of new tastes. Also, like my friend, people in general seem to have a certain image of Japanese food making them healthy, which is very appealing. This image is not without substance – it has arisen as a result of information relayed through various types of media.

The longevity of Japanese people also has something to do with this image. According to a report issued in 2010 by the Japanese Ministry of Health, Labor and Welfare, Japanese women live to an average age of 86.44 years and Japanese men to 79.59 years. These are the first and fifth longevity rankings, respectively, in the world. Even more surprising is that Japanese women have kept the top position for the past 25 years, while Japanese men have also ranked in the top longevity groups for the past 32 years.

There is another report that has helped enhance the image of the Japanese diet as being healthy. This report is generally known as the "McGovern Report" and was published in 1977 by the U.S. Senate Special Committee on National Nutrition, after spending a total of seven years and a great deal of money to complete it. This 5000 page report warned the American people that the chronic diseases they suffered from were primarily a result of their unhealthy diet. The report also pointed out that it was important to urgently reconsider what foods they should eat, listing seven guidelines for diet improvement. Moreover, it even referred to the diet Japanese people practiced 200 years ago as the best diet in the world. (At that time, the Japanese typically ate unpolished grain as their staple food with some side dishes of seasonal vegetables and sea products: including seaweed and small fish.) The report gave American people a strong impression that the Japanese diet is healthy even though it referred to the one 200 years ago.

There are other nutritional and statistical analyses and reports published by reliable public agencies which have led more and more people to believe that Japanese people probably live longer because of what they eat every day. These analyses strengthen the claims that the Japanese diet is good for people's health.

What Japanese people eat at home today is clearly different from what their ancestors ate 200 years ago. However, it is also a fact that there are more people aged eighty or over in Japan than in most countries across the world. Looking at this fact, it is not unreasonable to think that there are still some secrets even in the modern Japanese diet that may help Japanese people live so long. The modern Japanese diet still follows certain fundamentals of the traditional diet. From a nutritional viewpoint, it is also considered to be lower in both calories and fat than those of other countries. This suggests that the modern Japanese diet also contributes to the good health and consequent long life of modern Japanese people. Therefore, it is worthwhile to look into what secrets exist even in the modern Japanese diet.

Japanese people often use what other people think of as "yucky," food, such as raw fish and seaweed, for their everyday meals. They also drink green tea after almost every meal. But can people stay in good shape just by eating "yucky" food and drinking a few cups of green tea after that? Nutritionally, the Japanese diet is higher in carbohydrates and lower in animal fat and sugar than those of other developed countries. But does eating Japanese food automatically guarantee people a high-carbohydrate, low-fat and low-sugar diet?

The truth is, it is not that easy. The secrets are not only in the diet but also in Japanese food culture. Just like other countries' diets, the Japanese diet today has resulted from a tremendously long history of food culture. Superficial imitation of the diet without understanding the food culture will not actually teach us anything. What to eat is important of course, but that is not all. To learn how to keep good eating habits is just as important, for eating is something we must do everyday to survive and the benefits aren't as immediate as, say, medicine. Each generation of the Japanese people have followed their ancestors' wisdom (a certain way of eating, cooking, manner), consumed food, and contributed to the survival of their people. These habits have developed into the unique food culture that is cherished by so many contemporary Japanese people. The secrets of the healthy Japanese diet exist in the tradition of the Japanese food culture; that is, what and how they eat, and how they prepare their food.

It is therefore important to understand "the secrets of a healthy diet" that are hidden in Japanese food culture. I will explain the secrets from three different perspectives: (1) how Japanese people eat food; (2) how Japanese people cook food; and (3) what characterizes the Japanese people's eating habits.

1   How Japanese people eat

The most striking difference in food culture between Japan and the West is how they eat. Japanese eat food in a very unique way, which has been widely practiced in other countries across Asia. This unique way is called "*kochu-chomi*." In this way, people chew and mingle different kinds of food together to find their favorite tastes. Japanese people have kept this tradition of *kochu-chomi* for ages. Their staple food has been rice for thousands of years, which is usually steamed using only water. They eat steamed rice

alternately with seasoned side dishes. They somehow try to find the right balance between rice and the side dishes while mingling them in the mouth, and they savor the taste created by the perfect mixture of the food.

Side dishes eaten with steamed rice are generally called "*okazu*." They are eaten to supplement nutrients that rice doesn't provide, and to liven up the monotonous taste of plain rice. People living along the coast often eat sea products for their *okazu*, while those in the mountains eat vegetables from their fields. Mountain people also eat wild plants that are seasoned by salt, soy sauce, or soybean paste.

As far as cooking ingredients for *okazu* are concerned, Japan has been very lucky. Japan is blessed with a wide variety of ingredients because of the rich natural environment surrounding the land. If you take a look at a map, you can instantly realize that Japan is a tiny country located at the far eastern edge of Asia and is totally surrounded by the sea. This geographic feature has worked very well for Japanese people, bringing a lot of fresh fish to their dining tables. In particular, there are good fishery grounds on the Pacific side of the country, because a cold ocean current from the north (*Oya-shio*) and a warm current from the south (*Kuro-shio*) meet there and provide an optimal environment for so many different kinds of fish. In addition to those kinds of fish, other sea products from adjacent waters, including small-sized fish, shells, and seaweed have long been indispensable sources of protein and minerals for the Japanese diet.

Japan is also located in the monsoon region, in which the four seasons are

usually distinctive: summer is hot and wet and winter is cold and dry. Japan is especially hot and humid during the summer, which is suitable for rice plants to grow. This climate condition is good for other plants as well, and has made it possible to grow a diversity of agricultural products in the country.

These gifts from the rich natural environment around Japan made possible the unique way of eating called *kochu-chomi*, in which Japanese people eat unflavored steamed rice as "the staple food" and other seasoned food as "*okazu*." *Okazu* dishes are sometimes gifts from the sea, such as fish, shells, or seaweed, and sometimes gifts from the fields and mountains, such as vegetables and wild plants. Gifts from nature are seasonally different, and that affects *okazu* varieties. Japanese call seasonal ingredients "*shun-no-mono*," and they like to feel the transitions of the four seasons from them. This practice nurtures a sensitivity to and enjoyment of the seasons.

After World War II, Japanese food culture was exposed to a large measure of Western influence. Japanese people began eating Western-style dishes at home regularly, such as meat and dairy products, which had hardly been seen on dinner tables in Japan before. As a result, what Japanese people eat has gone through significant changes. However, the traditional way of eating, namely "*kochu-chomi*," has remained unchanged; Japanese still mostly eat just as their ancestors did a long time ago. It is true that the Western way of eating has been introduced and adopted by some people, but they account for a very small portion of the Japanese population. An overwhelming majority of them still consider meat, fish and vegetables to be cooked and seasoned as side dishes called "*okazu*," and rice as the staple food. In other words, Japanese people fill their stomachs with rice as the main carbohydrate and some "*okazu*" of meat, fish and vegetables on the side.

Japanese people draw a clear line between the staple food of rice and side dishes called "*okazu*." This unique way of eating results in a unique ratio in their food intake. That is, carbohydrates from rice accounts for a majority of the total intake and meat for a small percentage, meaning there is not too much animal fat.

2 How Japanese people cook

One of the unique things about Japanese cooking is how they use *umami*. This is a Japanese traditional culinary piece of wisdom that has helped Japanese people cook good-tasting food without oil.

Oil itself actually doesn't contain any component that human tongues can sense for any kind of taste. However, its richness and smoothness have magic powers to change ingredients into "good-tasting" food. There was virtually no edible oil in old Japan, and thus people used little oil for cooking. Instead, they used *umami* to flavor food.

Konbu

Generally, when people think that certain foods taste good, there is often a harmonized balance among the components of sweetness, saltiness, *umami*, sourness, and sometimes bitterness. Among those taste components, Japanese people have had a particularly strong interest in *umami* for ages. But what is *umami* anyway? Actually, nobody can answer that question clearly, but people all over the world have made use of it since ancient times. Broth and bouillon are a kind of *umami* extracted from meat and used in Western countries. Salted sardines called anchovies are another kind used mostly in countries around the Mediterranean Sea. Southeast Asian countries have their own fish sauces, made by fermenting fish. Each of these is a unique *umami* seasoning for a certain ethnic group and are used traditionally when cooking their ethnic foods.

umami used in Japanese cooking originates from dried kelp called "*konbu*" and flakes of dried bonito called "*katsuo-bushi*." *Konbu* is made by drying a kind of seaweed containing a lot of *umami*. *Katsuo-bushi* is made by boiling, fermenting and then drying bonito ("bonito" is a kind of tuna fish). Surprisingly, when combining these two kinds of *umami* ingredients, of plant- and animal-origins, an extremely rich flavor of *umami* is brewed. Japanese people call this extraction "*dashi*."

To make "*dashi*" is very easy. All it takes is to first soak *konbu* in a pot of water. After a while, put it on the stove and take the *konbu* out just before the water boils. Then, add thinly shaved *katsuo-bushi* to the water while it is boiling, turn the stove off, and wait for five to ten minutes. This is how to make Japanese traditional "*dashi*." Making "*dashi*" is relatively easier than making broth or bouillon, considering that all it takes is a little bit of time and just two kinds of ingredients. In traditional Japanese cooking, people have added flavor to foods containing little *umami* by using "*dashi*." But nowadays, instant *umami* cubes or powders both substitute for broth or bouillon and "*dashi*" in many kitchens.

Interestingly, "*dashi*" as a possible substitute for oil has also been proven through scientific experiments. Experimental results have shown that the mechanism by which "*dashi*" makes something taste good is the same mechanism by which oil does (Toru Fushiki, 2005*). Japanese people have been dependent to a great extent on this traditional "*dashi*" to cook good-tasting food without oil.

It was only a hundred years or so ago that science found a clear answer for the question of what "*dashi*" really was. Dr. Ikeda (1908), a Japanese scientist,

discovered that the main components of *umami* in *konbu* and *katsuo-bushi* were two kinds of amino acids, namely glutamic acid and inosinic acid. He also discovered that *umami* components in other ingredients were also a complex of various amino and nucleic acids. These components are generally found in meat and fish but sometimes in fermented dairy products like cheese and some vegetables like tomatoes and mushrooms. Later, a Japanese company successfully commercialized these *umami* components by using sugar cane as the main source and began selling it as *umami* seasoning all over the world.

Katsuo-bushi

Besides *konbu* and *katsuo-bushi*, fermented food is another source of *umami* in Japanese cuisine. The wide variety of fermented food is one of the characteristics of Japanese food. World-famous Japanese "*sushi*" is originally from "*nare-zushi*," which is a fermented food variation using rice and raw fish. Japanese traditional seasonings like soy sauce and *miso*, which is salty soybean paste, are also made through the fermentation of beans, wheat and rice. *Natto* (fermented soybeans), pickles, and dried fish are also made by fermenting grains, vegetables and fish. Honestly, many of these foods do not smell so good, but they taste wonderful. That is because microbes like lactic acid bacteria help the fermentation process in which the protein contained in the ingredients is partially decomposed into amino acids, the source of *umami*. There is no doubt that traditional Japanese fermented food has a lot to do with *umami*.

Another unique point in Japanese cooking is that ingredients do not go through a lot of complicated processes before being dished out. As mentioned, Japan is very lucky in terms of geography and climate, blessed with very productive mountains and seas as well as four distinctive seasons. It is surrounded by a rich natural environment that guarantees people very easy access to various foods, i.e., wild plants and vegetables (mountain products) and fish and shellfish (sea products), which are seasonal and always fresh. "*Shun-no-mono*," which is a general term for ingredients only available in a certain season, is especially considered the most delicious and nutritious when eaten at the height of their season. Japanese people feel the most appreciation for served dishes when they are "*shun-no-mono*," cooked in a simple way without losing their own natural taste and nutrients. Some people say that cooking in many countries can be characterized by "addition" because they produce delicious dishes by adding various seasonings, sauces and spices to original ingredients. Some say, on the other hand, that the Japanese-style cooking can be characterized by "subtraction." That is because original ingredients are processed using as little seasoning and sauces as possible to maximize their original taste and nutrition.

For example, there is a traditional dish called "*sashimi*" in Japan. Usually several kinds of raw fish are neatly arranged on a plate and dished out for people. *Sushi*, probably the most famous Japanese dish, actually uses pieces of *sashimi*, or raw fish. A *sushi* master puts a tiny piece of raw fish on a little cake of steamed rice that has been flavored with vinegar, sugar and salt. Because "*sashimi*" is raw fish, it can be considered to be the simplest dish requiring the least preparation. However, for the same reason, only certain kinds of fish can be used, and they also have to be very fresh. If you use the wrong kind of fish or neglect freshness, you will be very sorry and have to spend quite a long time in the bathroom. The trick to making good *sashimi* is to make the right judgment on the kind of fish and its freshness, and also knowing how to cut it with utmost skill. Eating *sashimi* of seasonal fish by dipping it into a little bit of soy sauce can be considered the simplest but yet most extravagant food. *Sushi* began as a gift from the rich natural environment around Japan, and has gained worldwide popularity.

Fresh, tasty, seasonal ingredients themselves are a feast to Japanese people, and because of that elaborate cooking using oil, sauces and other seasonings is not necessary. Eating like this is another important factor in keeping Japanese dishes low in calories and fat. Japanese dishes are said to be among the plainest in the world, but this tastelessness is a critical factor that contributes to Japanese people's health.

In sum, Japanese cooking is characterized by little oil, the skillful use of *umami* derived from *konbu* (dried kelp) and *katsuo-bushi* (flakes of dried bonito) or fermentation and the maximization of "taste," which innately exists in *shun-no-mono*, or seasonal, fresh ingredients. All of them contribute to the reputation of healthy Japanese food that is low in calories and fat.

3 What characterizes the Japanese people's eating habits

In Japan, people usually say "*itadakimasu*" with their heads down and their palms together before they start eating. This is nothing special. People all over the world have always done some kind of greeting or praying before they eat. People do it because they are well aware that they need food to support their lives.

In many developed countries, however, people nowadays rarely have special feelings when looking at the food before every meal. After World War II, Japan became one of the developed countries, and now very few Japanese often think about saying "*itadakimasu*" before every meal. None-theless, this word, to which the contemporary Japanese no longer pay much attention, is a symbolic one in which their ancestors embodied their special feelings toward food.

People who believe in a god probably pray, thanking God for the food, but "*itadakimasu*" does not imply any gratitude to a specific god. Instead, it is used to express gratitude to anything that exists and has life. Being at the top of the food chain, human beings can only sustain their lives at the sacrifice of a huge number of other living creatures, plants and animals alike. At every meal, Japanese people felt sorry for and grateful to countless lives having been sacrificed for them and reminded themselves that their existence depended solely on the precious blessing of other creatures' lives. By saying this word they also thanked everyone for the work put into preparing the meal. "*Itadakimasu*" is the word in which Japanese people try to express all those thoughts. Because of that, they may suffer from a sense of serious guilt when they cannot eat everything prepared for them, and use the word "*mottainai*" to express such a terrible feeling. This word means much more than just "waste." It implies some kind of affection Japanese people feel toward the leftovers. People have recently become aware that the global environment has gotten worse and have begun a global movement to protect the ecology. Reflecting on those words, the Japanese are one such group of people who have contributed to the idea of giving consideration to the protection of the environment and the ecology.

Since ancient times, Japanese people have not separated or differentiated themselves from nature, unlike their Western counterparts who have gradually separated themselves from other creatures. Rather, the Japanese have thought that everything in nature exists as a single network, with humans being just one part of it. They have regarded it as a virtue to be modest, thinking graciously that they are allowed to live by consuming other creatures' lives, symbolized by expressions such as "*itadakimasu*" or "*mottainai.*" In other words, to the Japanese it is important to harmonize oneself with the surrounding environment, be a part of nature or society, instead of establishing one's individuality and making the environment adjust to it, as seen in the West in general. This is the spirit of "*wa* (harmony)." It may not be too much to say that this spirit has been a major factor in maintaining the Japanese society. It is true that Japanese people tend to give the international community negative impressions of them, such as having few personal opinions or being indecisive, because of this unique spirit. It should also be noticed, however, that this spirit of "*wa*" has provided the foundation which allowed the Japanese people to build a safe, peaceful society for an unusually long period of time by global standards.

The globally long life expectancy of Japanese people is indeed attributed to physical factors, such as a well-balanced nutritious diet and advanced medical care and welfare. But also noteworthy is the "spiritual nutrition" that has helped Japanese people build and live in a safe, peaceful society based on the spirit of "*wa* (harmony)." Superficially, saying "*itadakimasu*" before every meal looks like just another habit in the Japanese diet culture, but it goes beyond that. It is based on the spirit of "*wa* (harmony)" on a deeper level, which has led to a safe, peaceful society. Japanese people may be unconsciously feeling how important *wa* is at every single meal, because if they don't harmonize small portions of various food derived from different part of nature in their mouth, they can't truly enjoy the meal.

I decided to publish this recipe book because I wanted many people to understand the Japanese diet better, instead of just having a general idea of a unique foreign diet using healthy ingredients.

For the book, I have carefully chosen ingredients that are readily available worldwide. The only exception I have made is with soy sauce and sake. These are easily found in many cities even outside Japan, and for that reason, they are used in many of the recipes in this book. Please note however that Japanese soy sauce is very different from Chinese soy sauce in taste and flavor and should be kept in the refrigerator, and that the sake used in the recipes is safe for children and those abstaining from alcohol, because the alcoholic content evaporates during cooking. No recipe requires any soup stock or *umami* seasoning at all; the ingredients themselves are the source of *umami*. Atmospheric pressure and water quality in different parts of the world can be minor factors that may have a subtle effect on cooking, but they are considered negligible in this book.

In the culinary culture of any county, there is a proud tradition that has contributed to the survival of the ethnic group. Such cultures deserve global respect as a cultural heritage. Fortunately, we now live in a time that lets us share the wisdom of other peoples that is hidden in such heritages. It is not easy to understand and accept each other's cultures. Clearly aware of that difficulty, however, I will be very happy if the wisdom hidden in the Japanese food culture helps other people even a little bit to become healthier and build a safe and peaceful society.

* Toru Fushiki, "Secrets of Richness and *Umami*," Shincho-sha Co. Ltd., Tokyo, 2005 (in Japanese).

Terms

Umami
A savory taste imparted by amino acids and nucleic acids, which occurs naturally in many foods, including meat, fish, dairy products, mushrooms and vegetables.

Kouchu-chomi
A way of eating in which people chew and mingle different kinds of food together in their mouth to find their own favorite tastes.

Okazu
Side dishes that are eaten with rice as a staple.

Konbu
Dried kelp, an ingredient essential for making dashi.

Katsuo-bushi
Flakes of dried bonito, an ingredient essential for making dashi.

Dashi
A soup stock that is made from konbu and katsuo-bushi.

Shun-no-mono
Seasonal food.

Wa
Japanese spirit as for harmony.

Alternatives

ゆず（*Yuzu*）

みそ（*Miso*）

中華めん（*Egg noodle*）

カツオ節（*Katsuo-bushi*）

Lemon

Pasta

Peanut butter and Japanese soy sauce

Canned tuna

Soup

Perhaps the most famous Japanese soup is *miso* soup. *Miso* is a very important Japanese seasoning that is made by fermenting soybeans with rice malt. For *miso* soup and other traditional Japanese soups, flakes of dried bonito called *katsuo-bushi*, dried small sardines called *niboshi* and dried *konbu* are used as essential ingredients in order to extract *umami* from them.

Since these ingredients are not always available outside Japan, some seafood, meat or vegetables rich in tasty amino and nucleic acids are used in the following recipes.

Clam soup
(*Ushio jiru*)

It is said the ancient Japanese ate a lot of shellfish. The evidence can be found at the many places where they once lived, now called *kaizuka*. The rich minerals and proteins contained in shellfish such as clams and oysters would have been a very important nutritional source for these ancient people.

Basically, *dashi* soup extracted from dried *konbu* and dried bonito is integral to the preparation of most Japanese soups. However, as for the soups containing shellfish as an ingredient, *dashi* soup is unnecessary because *umami* in the shellfish is extracted during cooking. While the method of preparation may be considered simple, it is very important to clean the shellfish thoroughly before cooking. Shellfish often have grit inside and this must be removed before they are cooked. The process is simple. Put the shellfish in salted water (3% salinity), cover with a cloth, and let it stand overnight. Shellfish exhale most of this grit during breathing. Failure to clean in them in this way may result in the soup having a gritty texture.

潮汁

Ingredients (4 servings)
3% salted water (2 1/2 teaspoons salt to 2 cups water) for pretreatment
18 oz (500g) clams
3 1/3 cups (800ml) water
2 tablespoons sake
1 teaspoon salt
2 teaspoons Japanese soy sauce
Fresh ginger slivered or lemon zest peeled thinly

Procedure
1.   Soak fresh clams in 3% salted water and let them stand still, covering with a cloth overnight in a dark place to let them expel sand. Wash well, rubbing shells against each other.
2.   Place the water and clams in a pan and cook over medium to high heat. Skim foam and season with sake and salt. Drizzle with Japanese soy sauce at the end.
3.   Throw away the unopened shells because they may have grit inside and serve only the opened clams and soup in bowls. Top with slivered ginger or thinly peeled lemon zest for flavor.

Green pea soup (vegetarian dish)

When we lose our appetite or have trouble swallowing food due to illness, a nutritious liquid diet is imperative to maintain our health. There are many kinds of soups smooth enough to swallow, such as vichyssoise, gazpacho, cream of vegetable soup and so on. In Japanese cooking, this kind of soup is called *suri-nagashi jiru*. *Suri* means grind, *nagashi* means pouring, and *jiru* means soup. Peas are rich in vegetable proteins and they are gently assimilated into the body. The butter added at the end makes the taste richer.

Ingredients (4 servings)
10 1/2 oz (300g) fresh or frozen peas
1 medium onion
2 cups (500ml) water
2 tablespoons sake
2 teaspoons salt
1 inch (2.5cm) on all sides butter

グリーンピーススープ

Procedure

1. Remove the fresh peas from the pods. If frozen, just remove from the packet. Cut the onion roughly.
2. Place the onion and the quantity of water in a pan, and cook over medium heat for a couple of minutes. Add the green peas (1), and after it starts boiling, put them into a blender with the liquid. Process for at least one minute and until smooth.
3. Put the soup (2) back into the same pan, and add the sake and salt. Cook over medium heat. After it is heated, turn off, add butter and serve in soup dish.

Chicken Tenderloin Soup
(*Tori-no-sasami jiru*)

If Western, Chinese and other methods of cooking are assumed to be the addition of ingredients, Japanese cooking may be said to be a subtraction of ingredients. Many Japanese dishes are simple and contain only those elements essential for taste and flavor. This soup may be said to express this essence of Japanese cooking. The taste is not complicated, but simple and enjoyable.

By simply tearing the tenderloin into thin strips, the texture is changed dramatically.

鶏ささみ汁

Ingredients (4 servings)
2 medium carrots
7 oz (200g) chicken tenderloins (about 3 pieces)
2/5 cup (100ml) sake
A pinch of salt
4 cups (1L) water
2 1/2 tablespoons Japanese soy sauce
Salt to taste

Procedure

1. Cut the carrot into 1-2 inch (2.5-5cm) lengths of thin juliennes.

2. Place the chicken in a pan, add sake and a pinch of salt. Cover with a lid and steam over a low heat.

3. When the chicken is cooked, take it out of the pan and cool. Tear into thin strips with your hands. Leave the liquid for the soup.

4. Add the quantity of water to the remaining soup (3), and then add the carrots (1) and the chicken (3). Bring it to a boil, remove any scum from the surface, and season with soy sauce. Add salt to taste.

Pork and Vegetable Soup
(*Buta jiru*)

This well-known soup is eaten in almost every Japanese home during the winter. *Umami* is released from both the pork and the vegetables. Soy sauce and peanut butter are used instead of *miso* here.

豚汁

Ingredients (4 to 6 servings)
7 to 10oz (200 to 300g) thinly sliced pork, belly or chuck
Salt
28oz (800g) vegetables in all
    Onions
    Leeks, white part only
    Carrots, peeled
    Cabbage leaves
    Mushrooms
    Potatoes, peeled
    Green beans
Sesame or vegetable oil
3 tablespoons sake
3 tablespoons Japanese soy sauce
1 1/2 tablespoons peanut butter
Salt
Finely slivered ginger
Red chili pepper (optional)

Procedure

1. Cut the pork and all of the vegetables into bite-sized pieces.
2. Heat the sesame or vegetable oil in a saucepan and sauté the pork until the fat renders out and turns lightly brown. Then add the onions, leeks, carrots, cabbage leaves, mushrooms, green beans and potatoes by turns and sauté over medium heat. Season with the Japanese soy sauce, sake and peanut butter, and sauté for a while. Pour on water until all the ingredients are immersed and cook over medium heat. After bringing it to a boil, skim off any scum from the surface.
3. When the potatoes are cooked, add salt or soy sauce to taste and serve in individual bowls. Top with finely slivered ginger and optionally sprinkle red chili pepper over it.

Japanese-style Chicken Soup
 (*Kashiwa jiru*)

There are many kinds of chicken soup in the world. As chicken contains a lot of *umami*, it is used as an important ingredient in many recipes. For convenience, the extract of whole chicken is concentrated and commercialized as soup stock or chicken bouillon. Although good soup can be made instantly by using these soup stocks, the taste seems more natural in soup made from fresh chicken rather than in that made with instant soup stock. By adding some types of vegetables, this chicken soup becomes an ideal and nutritious dish.

かしわ汁

Ingredients (4 servings)
10 1/2 oz (300g) boneless chicken thighs
1 teaspoon salt
1 medium carrot, peeled
3 medium cabbage leaves
2 medium potatoes, peeled
4 cups (1L) water
2 tablespoons sake
4 teaspoons Japanese soy sauce
Salt
Green sprouts or slivered lemon skin

Procedure

1.   Remove the fat particles from the chicken thighs and cut into bite-sized pieces. Sprinkle salt over the pieces, mix and leave for 15 minutes. Cut the vegetables into bite-sized pieces. Soak the potatoes in water in order to remove excess starch.

2.   Pat the chicken with kitchen paper or clean cloth to remove the liquid that comes out of chicken. Place the chicken (1), carrots, potatoes and water in a pan and bring to a simmer. Skim off any scum and extra oil from the surface. Add cabbage and sake. When all of the vegetables are cooked, add Japanese soy sauce for flavor and salt to taste. Serve in individual bowls and top with green sprouts or slivered lemon skin.

Meatball soup (*Niku-dango* soup)

Meatballs made from minced meat are soft to chew and easy to digest. This soup, made by combining meatballs and some types of vegetables, would be a nutritiously perfect meal for small children and elderly people who have small appetites. Meat acts as *umami*, so therefore it is unnecessary to add soup stock. The more you mix and knead the minced meat, the more elastic and soft it will become.

肉団子スープ

Ingredients (4 servings)

Vegetables

- 2 medium carrots, peeled
- 1 medium onion
- 4 medium mushrooms
- 3 1/2 oz (100g) snow peas, trimmed.

Meatballs

- 11 oz (310g) minced meat, pork or chicken
- 1/2 teaspoon salt
- Pepper
- 1 egg
- 2 tablespoons potato starch or cornstarch

4 cups (1L) water
1 teaspoon sugar (optional)
2 teaspoons salt
Pepper

Procedure

1. Cut the vegetables into bite-sized pieces.

2. *To make meatballs*: Place all the ingredients of the meatballs in a bowl. Knead it well and until sticky. Bring the quantity of water to a boil in a pan, and drop spoonfuls of mince mixture one by one into it and then simmer until cooked through.

3. Add carrots, onions, mushrooms and optionally sugar and skim any scum off the surface. When they are cooked, add the snow peas, and season with salt and pepper. Serve in soup dishes.

Rice and *Sushi*

Plain rice
(*Gohan*) (vegetarian dish)

Rice is the staple food of the Japanese people. We eat rice almost every day, and eat other foods such as eggs, fish, meat and vegetables as *okazu* (side dishes) with rice. By eating seasoned '*okazu*,' the plain taste of rice is complemented in the mouth.

Before steaming rice, we always wash rice several times in order to get rid of the remaining bran. This process is called '*togu*,' which means 'polishing' in Japanese. Using this word may help you imagine how important a food rice is to Japanese people. If you cannot find tasty rice in your area, just add one teaspoon (5ml) of vegetable oil for every 2 cups of short grain rice before cooking. The rice will become tasty.

ご飯

Ingredients (4 servings)
2 cups (480ml) short grain rice
2 cups plus 3 tablespoons (525ml) water
1 teaspoon (5ml) vegetable oil (optional when the quality of rice is not good)

Procedure

1. Place the rice in a big bowl, add ample water and swirl it around with your hand. Drain into a sieve and discard the milky water to remove the smell of bran. Repeat this action four to five times.

2. Place the rice in a heavy bottomed and deep saucepan and add the quantity of water (1.1 times to volume of rice). Leave it for 30 minutes to let it absorb water naturally. If the rice is not tasty, add the vegetable oil.

3. Heat it over high heat. When it starts boiling, cover with the lid. Put a piece of folded foil between the lid and the pot to let the steam out so that it will prevent the rice (with the hot water) from boiling and bubbling over from the pot. The foil should create a space about a quarter inch (0.5cm) space between the pot and the lid (see photo below) . Then turn the heat down to very low, and cook for a further 10 to 15 minutes. Then cover completely and turn off the heat. Leave undisturbed for a further 10 minutes to cook the rice with the remaining heat. If you use a rice cooker, this process will be done automatically.

4. Take off the lid and stir the rice gently from bottom to top, being very careful not to break the grains. Serve in individual bowls.

Plain rice balls
(*Omusubi*) (vegetarian dish)

Japanese people are fussy about the taste of rice. During the days when there was a shortage of rice, the target of rice breeding was mainly to increase yields. But in the 1950s, the supply of rice met the demands of the Japanese population, and so the main emphasis shifted to developing rice with good taste and texture, because people's desire changed from quantity to quality. Through the effort of breeders, rice varieties with required qualities, even when cooled were developed and these have spread throughout Japan. Now "*koshi-hikari*" is the most popular variety in Japan, because of its good quality and wide adaptability for cultivation. Plain rice balls are a dish for enjoying the taste of rice whether it is warm or cool. Rice does not affect the flavors of any other dishes which may be eaten with it. When making rice balls, be conscious of each grain and do not squash them with your hands.

Ingredients (4 servings)
6 cups plain rice (refer to the recipe for plain rice, page 41)
Salted water (2 teaspoons salt per quarter cup water)

Procedure

1. Dissolve the salt in the water. Wet palms with it, and take a large handful of warm rice. Make a flat ball or triangle by gently rolling in both hands.
2. Repeat this action with the remaining rice.

おむすび

Furikake Rice

When there is no "*okazu*" (side dish) for plain rice, some people sprinkle flakes called *furikake* over the rice. The ingredients for *furikake* are usually dried bonito flakes, roasted sesame seeds, dried eggs, dried seaweed, dried vegetables, etc. *Furikake* is made by combining these ingredients, which changes plain rice into a tasty dish. However it is very rare to make *furikake* at home, because many varieties are sold in supermarkets. This is a tested method of making *furikake* at home. The dried bonito flakes have been replaced by canned tuna, because this is available worldwide.

ふりかけご飯

Ingredients (10 servings)
3 1/2 oz (100g) canned tuna in water or brine
1 tablespoon mayonnaise
1 teaspoon sugar
1 teaspoon Japanese soy sauce
3 tablespoons roasted sesame seeds or finely chopped peanuts
Natural salt
Plain rice (refer to the recipe for plain rice, page 41)

Procedure

1.　Drain the canned tuna in a sieve. Place it in a pan and add mayonnaise, sugar and soy sauce. Heat over low and continue to stir with a wooden spoon or chopsticks until dry. Turn off the heat and dry with the remaining heat.

2.　Add the roasted sesame seeds or finely chopped peanuts and mix. Cool and add salt to taste. Sprinkle a couple of tablespoons of *furikake* over hot plain rice and serve. Store the leftovers in the refrigerator.

Baked Rice Balls

(*Yaki-onigiri*) (vegetarian dish)

焼きおにぎり

Rice balls (*onigiri*) are equivalent to sandwiches for Japanese people. We take them on picnics instead of sandwiches. Usually some kind of stuffing such as salted plum called *umeboshi*, salted salmon, or salted fish eggs, etc. are buried in a plain rice ball and shaped into a triangle or a round ball by hand. In order to prevent the rice grains from sticking to our hands when eating, *onigiri* is normally wrapped with dry seaweed called *nori*. Although *nori* is becoming a popular food as an ingredient of *sushi* rolls, here butter is used to prevent sticking. This international combination of western butter and eastern soy may, amazingly, whet your appetite.

Ingredients (4 servings)
2 cups (480ml) short grain rice
2 cups (480ml) water
2 tablespoons Japanese soy sauce
0.5 to 1 inches (1 to 2.5cm) cube of butter for cooking
Butter for frying

Procedure

1.   Wash the rice according to the recipe for plain rice (refer to the recipe for plain rice, page 41). Place the rice, water, soy sauce and the butter in a heavy bottomed pan, leave for 30 minutes, and cook over high heat. When it starts boiling, turn down the heat to very low, cover with a lid, put a folded piece of foil between the pot and the lid so that there is a space of about a quarter inch (0.5cm) between the lid and the pot to let the steam out and prevent it from bubbling over, and cook for 10 to 15 minutes. Turn off the heat, cover completely, and leave undisturbed for a further 10 minutes. Open the lid and stir gently from bottom to top, being careful not to break the rice grains. When you use a rice cooker, just put all the ingredients in the cooker and turn on the switch.

2.   Water both hands, and make round or triangle shaped rice balls, patting the two sides flat.

3.   Place as much butter as you like in a frying pan, and brown both sides of the rice balls (2) over low to medium heat.

Seasoned Rice (*Takikomi gohan*)

There are many kinds of seasoned rice dishes all over the world – Spanish paella, Indian *pulao*, the Middle Eastern *polow*, Greek *dolmathes*, American jambalaya, *arroz a la Mexicano*, African *jolof*, Asian fried rice and so on.

In Japan there are also many kinds of seasoned rice – mushroom rice, bamboo shoot rice, chestnut rice, seafood rice, mixed vegetable rice, seaweed rice, and so on. They are all called *takikomi-gohan*. Usually the recipe for *takikomi-gohan* is simple. You just add all the ingredients together and cook as usual with plain rice.

In this recipe, chicken is used as a main *umami* ingredient, and some vegetables are added. Japanese soy sauce usually plays an important role as a flavoring in most kinds of *takikomi-gohan*.

Ingredients (4 servings)
2 1/2 cups (600ml) short grain rice
2 cups plus 3 tablespoons (500ml) water
6 oz (170g) chicken breast skinless or tenderloin
Salt for pretreatment
7 oz (200g) mushrooms
3 1/2 oz (100g) carrots
3 tablespoons Japanese soy sauce
3 tablespoons sake
Chives or spring onions, finely chopped (optional)

炊き込みご飯

Procedure

1. Wash the rice according to the recipe for plain rice (refer to the recipe for plain rice, page 41), drain in a sieve and leave for 30 minutes. Slice the mushrooms thinly and cut the carrots into 1-inch (2.5cm) lengths of thin juliennes. Cut the chicken into small pieces, sprinkle a pinch of salt over them, mix and leave for 10 minutes.

2. Place the quantity of the rice (1) and water in a heavy bottomed pan or an electric rice cooker. Add the chicken, carrots, mushrooms (1), soy sauce and sake to the rice and mix lightly.

3. Cook over high heat until it starts to boil. When it starts boiling, turn down the heat to very low, cover with a lid, put a folded piece of foil between the pot and the lid so that there is a space of about a quarter inch (0.5cm) between the lid and the pot to let the steam out and prevent it from bubbling over, and cook for a further 10 to 15 minutes. Turn off the heat and leave completely covered for a further 10 minutes to help the moisture go into the middle of the grains using the remaining heat. Take off the lid and mix gently so that the grains are not broken up. Arrange in individual dishes. Top with the chives or spring onions optionally.

Crab Rice
(Kani meshi)

The northern part of Japan is a good fishing ground for crabs. Crabs have an extremely good taste, *umami*, but on the other hand, they are extremely expensive. As Japan is an island surrounded by oceans and has rich fishing grounds, the fishing industry is highly developed. Seafood has been a very important source of protein for the Japanese people and fish have been farmed since the 17th century. Nowadays Japanese knowledge and technology for fish farming are among the most advanced in the world. But unfortunately farming for crabs is rarely done because it takes too long to raise the crabs to commercial size, and it is not economical. So we just have to wait for the crabs to grow naturally in the sea. That is one reason why crabs are so expensive.

To Japanese people who lived mainly on seafood and rice, it was very natural to think of cooking the two together. This recipe is one example. If it's impossible to get fresh crab meat, canned crab can be used instead.

かに飯

Ingredients (4 servings)
2 1/2 cups (600ml) short grain rice
2 cups plus 1 tablespoon (500ml) water
2 tablespoons Japanese soy sauce
2 tablespoons sake
1 inch (2.5 cm) square cube of butter for cooking
7-10 oz (200-300g) boiled crab legs or a canned crab in water or brine
Butter for topping (optional)

Procedure

1. Wash the rice according to the procedure for plain rice (refer to the recipe for plain rice, page 41), drain in a sieve and leave for 30 minutes. Place the rice in a heavy bottomed and deep pan and add the quantity of water, Japanese soy sauce, sake and 1 inch (2.5 cm) square butter. When you use canned crab, drain and include the liquid in the total amount of water.

2. Cover with a heavy lid, put a folded piece of foil between the pot and the lid so that there is a space of about a quarter inch (0.5cm) between the lid and the pot to let the steam out and prevent it from bubbling over. Bring to a boil, then turn down the heat to very low and simmer. When the grains start to come out of the water, place the crab meat on top, put the lid back on and cook further. The total time required to cook is 10 to 15 minutes after the water starts to boil. Turn off the heat and leave for 10 minutes covering with the lid completely.

3. Take the crab meat out of the pot and set aside. Add butter to the rice as preferred and mix carefully so that the grains do not break. Serve in individual bowls and top with the crab meat.

Risotto (*Okayu*) and Poached Egg

For people whose digestive system is weakened by illness, a liquid or soft diet is the ideal. Japanese people eat plain risotto when they are weak and they give this to babies when they are being weaned because it is easily digested and allergic reactions to rice are rare. Here the poached egg is combined with plain risotto. If you like a runny yolk, keep the temperature of the water between 140 F (60 C) and 158 (70 C), because egg yolks and whites start to harden at 137 F (58 C) and 149 F (65 C), respectively. Japanese soy sauce drizzled over the soft eggs at the end is the perfect seasoning for this combination of eggs and rice.

Ingredients (4 servings)
4/5 cups (200ml) short grain rice
4 cups (1L) water
1/2 to 1 teaspoon salt
Poached eggs
   4 fresh eggs
   1 to 2 L water
Japanese soy sauce
Sesame or peanuts, ground
Spring onion or chives, finely chopped

Procedure

1. Wash the rice according to the recipe for plain rice (refer to the recipe for plain rice, page 41). Place the quantity of water and rice in a deep pan, and leave for 30 minutes. Cook over high heat, and when it comes to a boil, turn down the heat to very low. Cover with a lid, put a folded piece of foil between the pot and the lid so that there is a space of about a quarter inch (0.5cm) between the lid and the pot to let the steam out and prevent it from bubbling over, and cook for 15 to 20 minutes stirring with a spoon from time to time in order to prevent the grains from sticking to the bottom. When the rice thickens, add salt, turn off the heat, cover tightly and let it sit for 10 minutes.

2. *To make poached eggs*: Bring a pot of water to a boil, and turn off the heat. Break the egg into a small dish, and slide into the hot water. Put in the other eggs one by one, and cover with lid tightly. Leave for a while, and when the egg is cooked to desired doneness, take it out and transfer into a dish.

3. Divide the risotto (1) into serving bowls and place the poached egg (2) on top. Break the egg yolk using chopsticks, sprinkle on ground sesame or peanuts and spring onion and drizzle Japanese soy sauce over it when eating.

Three Colored Rice
(*San-shoku don*)

Small children like meals that are colorfully decorated. They do not eat a lot, but enjoy the meal with all their senses – sight, smell, taste, etc. This is one of the favorite dishes for small Japanese children. The colors are provided by eggs for yellow, peas for green, and chicken for brown. And of course, the white rice is hiding beneath them. Chicken flavored with ginger and soy sauce is an integral part of this meal. It would also be fun for children to help decorate the dish with colorful ingredients.

Ingredients (3 to 4 servings)

White part
  2 1/2 cups (600ml) short grain rice
  2 1/2 cups and 4 table spoons (660ml) water

Yellow part
  3 eggs
  2 teaspoons sugar
  2 teaspoons sake
  1/3 teaspoon salt
  Sesame or vegetable oil

Green part
  3 1/2 oz (100g) frozen or fresh peas
  A pinch of salt

Brown part
  8 oz (230g) minced chicken
  1 1/2 tablespoons sugar
  1 1/2 tablespoons sake
  1 1/2 tablespoons Japanese soy sauce
  1 tablespoon finely chopped fresh ginger
  Sesame or vegetable oil

三色丼

Procedure

1. *White part*: Cook rice according to the recipe for plain rice (page 41).

2. *Yellow part*: Combine the eggs, sugar, sake and salt in a bowl and mix well. Heat sesame or vegetable oil in a frying pan and pour in the egg mixture. Scramble it using four wooden chopsticks over a medium heat. Remove from heat from time to time and cook with the remaining heat while scrambling to crumble the eggs softly and finely. When the eggs are completely detached from the bottom of the pan, transfer on to a tray.

3. *Green part*: Put the frozen or fresh peas into boiling water with a pinch of salt. When the color turns bright green and the peas are fully cooked, drain in a sieve.

4. *Brown part*: Season the chicken with sugar, sake, Japanese soy sauce and finely chopped ginger in a bowl. Heat the sesame or vegetable oil in a frying pan and scramble the chicken using four wooden chopsticks to make the chicken crumble finely. Remove from the heat from time to time while scrambling to make the chicken soft. When cooked through and the liquid is almost evaporated, spread in a tray.

5. Divide the cooked rice (1) in individual dishes or bowls. Arrange the eggs (2), peas (3) and chicken (4) nicely on top of the plain rice.

Sushi Salad

寿司サラダ

Sushi has become an international food nowadays. But it is still considered something to be served at Japanese restaurants or *sushi* shops. Can it become a more familiar food that can be done by anyone, anywhere? This recipe was created based on this question.

Basically the rice used in *sushi* is seasoned only with rice vinegar, sugar and salt. If vegetable oil is added to this seasoning, it has almost the same components as a salad dressing. So, here rice is seasoned with a sweet dressing originating from *sushi* seasoning, mixed with fresh salad, ham and cheese, and flavored with citrus. If more rice is added to the salad, it could be served as a healthy and filling main dish.

Ingredients (3 to 4 servings)
Sushi dressing sauce
    1 tablespoon rice or apple vinegar
    1 tablespoon juice of orange
    1 tablespoon juice of lemon
    1 1/2 tablespoons sugar
    1 teaspoon salt
    1 tablespoon vegetable oil
Rice
    2 cups (480ml) medium short grain rice
    2 cups (480ml) water
4 asparagus
1 continental or 2 Lebanese cucumbers
1 avocado
7 oz (200g) ham
7 oz (200g) natural cheese
Lettuce
1 lemon zest, finely slivered
Fresh ginger, finely slivered

Procedure

1. *To make sushi dressing sauce*: Combine the rice or apple vinegar, juices of orange and lemon, sugar, salt, and stir until the sugar and salt are dissolved. Drip in the vegetable oil little by little, stirring to emulsify the liquid and oil.

2. *To cook rice*: Cook the rice with the quantity of water according to the procedure for plain rice (refer to the recipe for plain rice, page 41). When cooked, leave for 5 to 10 minutes covering with the lid. Put the rice into a large bowl and pour the *sushi* dressing sauce (1) over the hot rice. Mix carefully so that the grains are not squashed.

3. Chop off the woody part of asparagus, and parboil in salted water. When the color turns bright green, drain in a sieve and cut into 1 inch (2.5cm) pieces. Cut the cucumber, avocado, ham and cheese into 1/2 inch (1cm) cubes. Put the avocado in the lemon juice to prevent oxidization. Tear the lettuce into favorite sized-pieces by hand.

4. When the rice (2) is cooled, add the asparagus, cucumber, ham and cheese, finely slivered lemon zest and ginger, and mix by hands or using a large spoon. Spread lettuce in a large dish and place the *sushi* mixture on the lettuce. Top with avocado and serve.

Sushi Balls
(Nigiri zushi)

にぎり寿司

The *sushi* served in a Japanese restaurant is usually *nigiri-zushi*, which has raw fish on the top of small amounts of shaped rice. But it is difficult to make good *nigiri-zushi* at home, because it requires the special techniques of a professional *sushi* chef. Here their technique is imitated by using cling film. The ingredients for *sushi* can be anything you like – seafood, meat or vegetables. Enjoy making *nigiri-zushi* with your family or friends by placing a big bowl of *sushi* rice, a plate full of your favorite foods, Japanese soy sauce, and cling film in the middle of the table.

Ingredients (4 servings)

Rice

    3 cups (720ml) short grain rice

    3 cups (720ml) water

Sushi seasoning

    2/5 cup (100ml) rice or apple vinegar

    2 tablespoons sugar

    1 teaspoon salt

Homemade teriyaki sauce

    1 tablespoon Japanese soy sauce

    1 tablespoon sake

    1 tablespoon sugar

Examples of topping foods –

*Steamed chicken (refer to the recipe for *Sake Liqueur-steamed Chicken*, page 81), thinly sliced cucumber and homemade *teriyaki* sauce

*Roast beef, ground ginger or horseradish and homemade *teriyaki* sauce

*Avocado with soy sauce, prawns and mayonnaise

*Sashimi-grade tuna or salmon and chopped chives

*Slices of smoked salmon, cheddar or cream cheese and thinly sliced onion (soaked in water for at least for 20 minutes and dried)

*Chopped ham or canned tuna, cheese and thinly sliced cucumber

*Imitation crab and green sprouts Japanese soy sauce

*Fried chicken and a slice of lemon or lime

Wasabi (optional)

A small bowl of water or vinegar to wet a tablespoon for scooping *sushi* rice

Procedure

1.   *To make sushi rice*: cook the rice with the quantity of water according to the recipe for plain rice (refer to the recipe of plain rice, page 41). Combine the ingredients for sushi seasoning. When the rice is cooked, leave for 10 minutes, covering with the lid and then tip over the rice in a large bowl. Pour the sushi seasoning over the hot rice, and mix it, being careful not to squash the grains.

2.   *To make homemade teriyaki sauce*: Place all the ingredients in a small skillet and heat over a low heat. As soon as the sauce begins to simmer and thicken, immediately remove it from the heat.

3.   Wash hands and spread the cling film on a flat board or plate. Place about one tablespoon of rice on the film and wrap it up. Twist the both ends of the film so that it appears like a candy (see the photo above). After shaping the sushi rice like a sushi ball, take the film off and put a slice of your favorite ingredient on top of the sushi rice. If you like spicy food, add a bit of wasabi between the topping and the rice. Wrap it up tightly in the same cling film again to make the both stick together and shape into oval or round like sushi. You can also wrap the sushi ball with thin slices of cucumber and put ham and/or cheese or something favorite on top of the rice (see the photo in page 58). Remove the cling film, wet the tablespoon for sushi rice with water or vinegar and repeat the same process with other toppings. Top with homemade *teriyaki* sauce or mayonnaise for preference.

4.   Hold the sushi balls with your fingertips, dip the tip of the ball in fresh Japanese soy sauce and eat.

*Note 1: People tend to make sushi balls in large size when hungry. But large sushi balls are hard to be brought to the mouth from the dish and easy to fall apart when eating. Keep in mind to always make mouthful size of sushi.

Note 2: If you are not good at making small sushi balls or feel that it is troublesome, place the sushi rice in an individual bowl and decorate the top with your favorite ingredients. It becomes a lovely *chirashi-zushi*.

Colorful *Sushi*
(Chirashi zushi)

ちらし寿司

At home, we usually make *sushi* rolls or *chirashi-zushi*, because out of the many kinds of traditional *sushi*, *chirashi-zushi* seems to be the easiest one to make. *Chirashi* means spreading or decorating, and *zushi* means *sushi*. So *chirashi-zushi* is a *sushi* colorfully decorated with different types of food, for example eggs (yellow), prawns (red), snow peas (green), etc., placed on top of the *sushi* rice. You can serve this in a large bowl and then divide it into individual dishes or you can make *sushi* in individual bowls.

Ingredients (4 servings)

Seafood for *red color*
- Boiled prawns, crab meat, smoked salmon, canned crab meat or imitation crab.

Scrambled egg for *yellow color*
- 4 eggs
- 1/3 teaspoon salt
- 1 tablespoon sake
- 1 teaspoon sugar
- Sesame or vegetable oil

Green vegetables for *green color*
- Snow peas, asparagus, cucumber and/or avocado

Sushi rice
- 3 cups (720ml) rice
- 3 cups (720ml) water
- 1/3 cup (80ml) rice or apple vinegar
- 2 tablespoons sugar
- 1 teaspoon salt
- 3 tablespoons roast sesame or finely chopped peanuts.

Vegetable mixture to season sushi rice
- 1 1/2 medium carrots
- 5 medium mushrooms
- 2 tablespoons Japanese soy sauce
- 1 tablespoon sugar
- 2 tablespoons water
- 1 small knob of fresh ginger, peeled and slivered

Procedure

1. *To cook seafood for red color*: Remove the shells from the prawns and cut them in half lengthways, or take the crab meat out of the shell. When you use canned crab, drain the liquid. When using imitation crab meat, tear it lengthwise, and when using ham or smoked salmon, slice into bite sized pieces.

2. *To make scrambled eggs for yellow color*: Place the eggs, a pinch of salt, sake and sugar in a bowl and beat. Heat sesame or vegetable oil in a frying pan and pour in the egg mixture. Scramble it using four wooden chopsticks over a low heat and remove from the heat from time to time in order to cook with the remaining heat. Keep scrambling until the eggs are cooked finely.

3. *To cook green vegetables for green color*: Take off the strings of the snow peas. Bring a small pan of salted water to a boil and blanch the snow peas and/or asparagus. Take them out when the color turns bright green. If you use cucumber and/or avocado, cut into 1/2 inch (1cm) cubes.

4. *To make sushi rice*: Cook rice with the quantity of water according to the recipe for plain rice (refer to the recipe for plain rice, 41). Combine the ingredients for sushi seasoning. When the rice is cooked, leave for 10 minutes covering tightly, and then tip over in a large bowl. Pour the sushi seasoning over the hot rice, and mix it, being careful not to squash the grains. Add the roast sesame seeds or finely chopped peanuts and mix.

5. *To make vegetable mixture to season sushi rice*: Cut the carrots into 2 inch (3cm) thin strips and slice the mushrooms. Put them in a saucepan, and add the Japanese soy sauce, sugar and water. Heat over medium and remove any scum from the surface. When the liquid is nearly evaporated, turn off the heat and add the thinly slivered fresh ginger. Add to the sushi rice (4), and mix carefully so that the grains do not break up.

6. Serve in a large dish and decorate the top nicely with eggs (yellow) (2), vegetables (green) (3) and seafood (red) (1). Divide into individual dishes when eating.

Pasta, Noodles and Pancakes

The most popular and traditional Japanese noodles are *udon* and *soba*. *Udon* is made from wheat flour, and *soba* is made from wheat and buckwheat flours. They are eaten either hot or cold with soup, which is basically made from *dashi*, soy sauce, *mirin* (sweetened sake), and sugar. But here Italian pastas are used instead of these, because Japanese noodles are not available worldwide.

When we eat noodles, we follow Japanese table manners. A noise must be made when slurping noodles. As well as tasting with our mouths, seeing with our eyes and smelling with our noses, hearing with our ears is also considered to be an element of enjoying delicious foods. This is why we make slurping noises when we eat noodles. But this manner of eating is limited to noodles and there is, of course, a certain way to make the correct kind of slurp when eating.

In this chapter, pancakes made from flour and vegetables are added.

Cold Noodles
(*Reimen*)

The summer in Japan is very hot and humid, and people tend to lose their appetite. Therefore, people prefer to eat cold noodles during the hot season, because of its smooth and cold feeling when passing through the throat. Japanese cold noodles such as *somen*, *hiyamugi*, *udon* and *soba* are used in this dish, but the thinnest spaghetti, *capellini*, would be a good replacement for these. If you put plenty of fresh salad on the noodles, this dish would become a good pasta salad.

Ingredients (3 to 4 servings)
Sauce
   1/4 cup (60ml) Japanese soy sauce
   1/2 cup (120ml) water
   2 tablespoons sugar
   2 tablespoons lemon or lime juice
   2 tablespoons vegetable oil
   1 tablespoon sesame oil (optional)
Vegetables
   Fresh ginger, slivered thinly
   1 medium carrot
   1 continental or 2 small Lebanese cucumbers
   Alfalfa and/or green sprouts
11 oz (300g) spaghetti, *capellini*
7 oz (200g) *sakamushi* chicken and its liquid
   (refer to the recipe for *Sake Liqueur-steamed Chicken*, page 81) or canned tuna
Roasted sesame seeds or finely chopped almonds

冷
麺

Procedure

1. *To make sauce*: Place the soy sauce, water, sugar, lemon or lime juice in a large bowl, and dissolve the sugar by stirring. Drop in the vegetable oil and optionally the sesame oil little by little, stirring with a whisk in order to emulsify the liquid with the oil. Add thinly slivered fresh ginger and mix.

2. Cut the carrots and cucumbers into julienne strips as thinly as possible.

3. Cook the spaghetti according to the instructions on the package. Prepare a large bowl of ice water. When the noodles are cooked, drain in a sieve, and plunge them into the ice water to prevent overcooking. Drain well and add into the sauce (1). Combine the noodles and sauce using tongs, and transfer into individual dishes.

4. Top with plenty of vegetables and thinly torn *sakamushi* chicken with its liquid or canned tuna. Pour on the remaining sauce and top with sesame seeds or finely chopped almonds.

Mushroom Spaghetti
(*Wafu kinoko spaghetti*) (vegetarian dish)

Spaghetti is a famous Italian noodle, which is popular all over the world. In Japan, Italian dishes called *ita-meshi* (*ita* means Italian and *meshi* means meal) enjoyed a boom a couple of decades ago, and today they are still one of the most popular meals. Noodles, especially spaghetti, whetted the Japanese people's appetite because of their comfortable and smooth feeling in the mouth and throat. Though there are so many kinds of original Italian recipes for pasta, some new recipes were invented by Japanese chefs by using new ingredients – soy sauce, *miso*, fish eggs, dried fish, seaweed, Japanese herbs and other Japanese specific ingredients.

Japanese people are excellent at innovating or changing things that are imported from foreign countries in many areas to make them more convenient or more suitable to Japanese tastes. This seems to be one facet of traditional Japanese culture. This recipe is an example of how foreign foods can be modified to suit the Japanese culinary culture.

Though dried seaweed called *nori* and a Japanese herb called *shiso* are usually sprinkled on top of this dish, chives, chopped spring onion or parsley leaves can be used instead.

きのこスパゲティ

Ingredients (2 servings)
2 cloves of garlic
1 red chili pepper
11 oz (310g) mushrooms
4 oz (100g) oyster mushrooms
7 oz (200g) spaghetti
Olive oil
1 tablespoon Japanese soy sauce
1 inch (2.5cm) cube of butter
Salt and pepper
Chives, spring onions, or parsley, finely chopped

Procedure

1.   Crush the garlic. Take the seeds out of the red chili pepper and cut thinly using scissors. Slice the mushrooms. Trim the stems from the oyster mushrooms and tear into small clusters.

2.   Cook the spaghetti until *al dente* according to the package instructions.

3.   While the spaghetti is cooking, heat the olive oil over low in a wok or a frying pan, and add the garlic (1). Heat slowly, and when the aroma is released, take the garlic out of the pan, and add the chili and all of the mushrooms (1). Cook over medium heat, and when the liquid starts coming out of the mushrooms, add the Japanese soy sauce. Turn off the heat and set aside.

4.   When the spaghetti is cooked until *al dente*, drain in a sieve, and combine with the hot mushroom sauce (3) and the butter. Serve in a dish and sprinkle chopped chives, spring onions or parsley on top.

Japanese Fried Noodles

(*Shio yakisoba*)

Many Japanese people who live overseas miss the taste of *yakisoba*, which is a stir-fried noodle seasoned mainly by Japanese Worcestershire sauce. They are one of the most popular Japanese foods, and are sold at stalls on festival days and at food courts in shopping malls in general. But unfortunately it is difficult to get *yakisoba* noodles and *yakisoba* seasoning outside of Japan. So in this recipe, the noodle is replaced by spaghetti, *linguine*, and seasoning is done only with salt and pepper. *Umami* from pork belly and the flavor of ginger are harmonized in the mouth.

塩焼きそば

Ingredients (4 servings)
10 1/2 oz (300g) thinly sliced pork belly or chunk
1/4 head medium cabbage
2 green peppers
9 oz (250g) bean sprouts
11 oz (300g) spaghetti, *linguine*
3 tablespoons sesame oil or vegetable oil
1/2oz (15g) fresh ginger, finely slivered
Salt and black pepper

Procedure

1.   Cut the pork and cabbage into bite-sized pieces. Slice the green peppers thinly. Wash the bean sprouts and drain in a sieve.

2.   Cook the spaghetti until *al dente* according to the package instructions. Prepare a large bowl of ice water and set aside. When the spaghetti is cooked, drain and plunge into the ice water in order to stop overcooking. When cooled down, drain well in a sieve and set aside.

3.   Heat the sesame or vegetable oil in a wok or large frying pan, add the pork and cook over medium heat. When the fat renders out and the color turns lightly brown, add the cabbage, green pepper and bean sprouts (1), and stir fry them quickly over high heat. Before the liquid comes out of the vegetables, add the spaghetti (2) and ginger, and sprinkle the salt and black pepper. Combine, and when the noodles are fried, serve in individual dishes.

Japanese Noodle Soup
(*Ramen*)

Ramen is a very popular Japanese dish throughout the world nowadays. However, it originated from Chinese noodles, and its soup stock has basically been extracted by simmering legs of pork with ginger and leeks. In order to avoid the laborious process, MSG is often used instead like instant cup ramen noodles. In this recipe, curly *ramen* noodles are replaced by the thinnest kind of spaghetti, *capellini*, and the soup is extracted from salted pork meat instead of legs of pork. Eating it while it is hot is recommended, because the noodles will absorb the soup, and become thick and soft as time goes by.

Ingredients (2 servings)
18 oz (500g) pork chuck or loin
2 teaspoons salt
Water
1 oz (30g) ginger
1 leek, cut into 4 inch (10cm) lengths
1 teaspoon sugar
2 tablespoons Japanese soy sauce
Salt to taste
7 oz (200g) spaghetti *capellini*
7 oz (200g) bean sprouts, washed and drained
Spring onions, chopped
White pepper
Sesame oil (optionally)

Procedure

1. Tie the chunk of pork with a string. Put it in a plastic bag and add the salt. Rub so that the salt covers the meat evenly. Keep it for 2 or 3 nights in the refrigerator.

2. Place the pork (1), ginger and leek in a deep pan and pour on water until the pork is completely immersed. Simmer it over low heat, covering with a lid for one hour until softened. Remove from the heat, and leave the pan until cooled down enough to handle. Take the pork out of the pan, untie the string, and cut into 1/2 inch (1cm) thicknesses and set aside.

3. Drain the remaining soup in a sieve to remove the ginger, leek and debris, and place it in a large pan. Add the sugar, Japanese soy sauce and salt to taste. Reheat it before serving.

4. Cook the spaghetti *capellini* according to the instructions on the package and transfer into a large serving bowl using a tong. Add the bean sprouts into the hot remaining water where the spaghetti has been cooked, and drain in a sieve immediately when heated.

5. Reheat the soup (3) and pour it over the noodles in serving bowls (4). Top with bean sprouts (4), pork slices (2) and chopped spring onions, and sprinkle white pepper. If you wish, add a few drops of sesame oil as a flavor. Serve while it is hot. Keep the leftover meat in refrigerator for another meal such as a salad or sandwich.

Veggie-Pancakes
(*Okonomi -yaki*)

Wheat and barley were originally cultivated as a second crop of grain for winter in Japan. In the Japanese custom of eating grain whole rather than grinding, the threshed grains of barley were mixed and steamed with rice. This dish is called *mugi-meshi*. On the other hand, grains of wheat were also ground into flour and used mainly in noodles called *udon*, *somen*, *hiyamugi*, and so on.

Okonomi-yaki is a local dish using flour that was created in the southwest area (*Osaka and Hiroshima*) of Japan. *Okonomi* means your favorite and *yaki* means cooking. So *okonomi-yaki* means a dish where any ingredients that you like, such as any meat, seafood or vegetables, are mixed with flour and cooked in a frying pan. Usually cabbage is the main ingredient and meat or seafood is added to it. The key to making these pancakes taste so good is the *okonomi-yaki* sauce that is spread on top after cooking. Here, a *okonomi-yaki* sauce is made using English Worcestershire sauce, ketchup and mayonnaise.

Ingredients (4 servings)
Okonomi-yaki sauce
    1 tablespoon Worcestershire sauce
    2 tablespoons ketchup
    2 tablespoons mayonnaise
7 oz (200g) canned tuna in water or brine
1/3 to 1/2 head cabbage, cut into slivers
1 zucchini, cut into slivers
1/2 teaspoon salt
2 teaspoons sugar
4 eggs
1 cup (240ml) flour
Vegetable oil
Dry parsley or green tea leaves smashed by coffee mill for preference

お好み焼き

Procedure

1. *To make okonomi-yaki sauce*: Combine all the ingredients in a bowl.

2. *To make batter*: Place the canned tuna with liquid, cabbage, zucchini, salt, sugar, eggs and flour in a bowl, and mix until smooth.

3. Heat the vegetable oil in a frying pan. Scoop the batter (2) in a ladle and spread into a round shape, about 6 inches (15cm) diameter and cook over low to medium heat.

4. When the bottom is cooked, turn it over and cook on the other side. But never press the pancake with a turner. Serve on a plate with *okomomi-yaki* sauce (1) and cut into some pieces. Repeat the same action for the rest of the batter. When you eat, spread the sauce on the top of each pancake, or dip the piece of pancake in the sauce. Sprinkle with dry parsley or smashed green tea leaves over the top, as preferred.

Chicken and Eggs

Chicken Kebab

(*Yakitori*)

Chicken itself has a good *umami*. *Yakitori* is one of the good ways to get the real taste of the chicken. Cut the chicken into small pieces, put them on bamboo skewers and sprinkle with salt, then grill or BBQ. The surplus oil and liquid come out of the chicken and the *umami* will be concentrated in this. Plus the lovely smell of smoke will be added to the chicken if it is cooked using charcoal.

This dish is good with drinks, but is also loved by children. The bite-sized chicken and the sweet flavor that comes from *teriyaki* sauce may satisfy their appetite. Please be careful not to prick your fingers when you skewer the small pieces of chicken, and never forget to take the chicken pieces off the skewer before serving small children.

Ingredients (2 to 3 servings)
Yakitori sauce
  1/5 cup (50ml) Japanese soy sauce
  1 tablespoon sake
  1 tablespoon sugar
18 oz (500g) boneless chicken thighs and/or breasts
Bamboo skewers

Procedure
1. *To make yakitori sauce*: combine all the ingredients.
2. Cut the chicken into bite-sized pieces. Marinate them in *yakitori sauce* (1) for 10 minutes. Thread them onto skewers and wrap the rest of the skewers with aluminum foil to avoid burning.
3. Grill them until golden brown on a barbecue or under a grill. If you do not have either of these, heat a little vegetable oil in a non-stick frying pan, and cook the chicken on both sides.
4. Take off the foil, and arrange them on a serving plate to share.

Japanese Omelet
(*Tamago-yaki*)

In Japan, there are some traditional recipes made of eggs, such as *dashi-maki-tamago*, *chawan-mushi*, *tamago-dofu*, *tamago-donnburi* and so on. In most of them, *dashi*, which is a soup stock extracted from dried *konbu* and flakes of dried bonito, is used as an essential ingredient.

Here a very simple recipe that can be made without *dashi* is shown. Leeks are used as an ingredient providing *umami*, flavor and sweetness to the eggs. Although *tamago-yaki* is originally a rolled omelet, if it is difficult to roll the omelet in the frying pan, simply cook both sides of the omelet in heated oil.

Ingredients (2 servings)
Lettuce
Tomatoes
2 to 3 oz (60 to 85g) leek, only white and soft parts or spring onions
4 medium eggs
2 teaspoons Japanese soy sauce
2 teaspoons sake
1/2 teaspoon sugar
Sesame or vegetable oil

Procedure

1. Wash and tear the lettuce by hand. Cut the tomatoes into bite-sized pieces. Arrange the lettuce and tomatoes in individual serving dishes. Slice the leek or spring onions very thinly.

2. Beat the eggs in a bowl. Add Japanese soy sauce, sake, sugar and leeks or spring onions (1), and mix.

3. Heat the sesame or vegetable oil in a frying pan over medium heat. Pour a ladle of the egg mixture (2) and make omelet using a turner to cook on both sides. Transfer onto the serving dish arranged with lettuce and tomatoes (1) and serve. Repeat the same procedure for the remaining egg mixture.

たまご焼き

Sake Liqueur-steamed Chicken with Cucumber

(*Tori-no-saka-mushi*)

鶏の酒蒸しのきゅうり和え

Saka-mushi is one of the traditional methods of Japanese cooking. *Saka* means sake liqueur made from rice and *mushi* means steaming. So *saka-mushi* means food steamed with sake. Generally speaking, the alcohol in the liqueur helps erase the unwanted smell of ingredients and adds a flavor. By steaming the chicken with sake or other liqueur, the unwanted smell evaporates along with the alcohol and the good flavor remains to be added to its original *umami*. Chicken tenderloin is the part that has less fat than any other part of the chicken. The flavor and acid of fresh citrus juice and slivers of thinly sliced fresh cucumber make the chicken taste fresh and cool. The process of removing the liquid from the fresh cucumber using salt is necessary to combine the chicken and fresh vegetables. Keeping the dish cool in a refrigerator just before serving is recommended.

Ingredients (4 servings)
6 oz (170g) tenderloin chicken, about 4 pieces
1/5 cup (100ml) sake
1/2 teaspoon salt
1 continental or 2 small Lebanese cucumbers
1 teaspoon salt
4 tablespoons fresh orange juice
1 tablespoon lemon or lime juice
Small pieces of lemon or lime zest

Procedure

1.   Place the chicken in a saucepan, and add sake and salt. Cover the pan and heat over low. Steam it for about a couple of minutes and remove from the heat to cook them with the remaining heat.

2.   Cut the cucumber into thin julienne strips, sprinkle with salt, mix and leave for 10 minutes. Squeeze out any excess liquid by hand.

3.   After the chicken pieces (1) become cool enough to handle, remove from the pan and tear them along the fiber into thin pieces using your fingers. Place the chicken in a bowl and add the fresh orange juice and lemon or lime juice, and mix.

4.   Add the cucumber (2) and toss. Serve in a dish and top with a small piece of the lemon or lime zest.

Chicken and Eggs with Rice
(Oyako don)

Japanese people love dishes known as *donburi* or *don*. In these dishes, the rice and main meal are served together in a large rice bowl. The rice is put at the bottom and the main dish served on top of it. *Oyako don* is commonly served at home and translates as "parent and child," suggesting the relationship between the chicken and the egg.

Ingredients (2 to 3 servings)
6 oz (200g) boneless chicken thigh or breast
A pinch of salt
1/2 teaspoon potato starch or cornstarch
Vegetable oil
1 medium onion, thinly sliced
1 tablespoon sake
1 teaspoon sugar
2 tablespoons Japanese soy sauce
1/3 cup (80ml) water
4 medium eggs, lightly beaten
Frozen green peas
3 cups plain rice, hot cooked
(refer to the recipe for plain rice, page 41)

親子丼

Procedure

1.   Slice the chicken thinly at a steep angle to make wide slices and cut into bite-sized pieces. Place the chicken and a pinch of salt in a bowl and mix. Add potato starch or cornstarch to make the texture of the chicken soft, then mix well by hand.

2.   Heat vegetable oil in a non-stick frying pan and sauté the chicken. When cooked, take them out and set aside.

3.   Add the vegetable oil into the same pan and sauté the onion until lightly brown. Bring back the chicken (2) into the pan and add sake, sugar, Japanese soy sauce and water. Bring it to a boil, then evenly pour the half of lightly beaten eggs over them and heat until cooked, moving the frying pan from time to time. But never stir the eggs. Pour the remaining eggs over them and top with green peas. Then turn off the heat and cover with a lid in order to cook the eggs with the remaining heat until your desired doneness.

4.   Arrange the hot plain rice in individual bowls, and transfer the chicken and egg mixture (3) over the rice using a ladle. Serve with a spoon or chopsticks.

Teriyaki Chicken

In *teppan-yaki* restaurants overseas, the chefs often entertain their guests. The food is cooked in front of the customers on a huge iron grille called a *"teppan"*. The chef will throw the foods into the air and then serve it immediately onto each guests' waiting plate. This performance is designed to entertain and provide enjoyment. However in Japan, it is not considered good manners to play with food in this way.

A sweet soy sauce called *teriyaki* is served in *teppan-yaki* restaurants. Although it is possible to buy *teriyaki* sauce in supermarkets in some countries, the taste is quite different to that of the original. True *teriyaki*-sauce is made from only Japanese soy sauce, sake and *mirin* (sweetened sake). These are all fermented seasonings and they provide a less sweet taste than the commercial sauces.

In this recipe, *teriyaki* chicken is cooked in a small pan at home rather than in a *teppan-yaki* restaurant. An original *teriyaki* sauce recipe is used to provide a true Japanese taste. Don't be tempted to throw the chicken into the dish. This is obviously dangerous!

鶏
の
照
り
焼
き

Ingredients (4 servings)
21 oz (600g) boneless and skinned chicken thighs,
    cut into 2-3 inch (5-7.5cm) pieces
Salt and pepper
 Vegetable oil
Teriyaki sauce
    2 tablespoons Japanese soy sauce
    2 tablespoons sake
    1 tablespoon sugar
    2 tablespoons water
Lettuce
Lemon or lime, sliced

Procedure

1.   Remove excess fat particles from the chicken. Cut into 2 to 3 inch (5 to 7.5cm) pieces so that the chicken can be easily cooked thoroughly, lightly season with salt and pepper and leave for 10 minutes.

2.   Pat the chicken pieces with a clean cloth or kitchen paper to remove the liquid on the surface. Heat the vegetable oil in a non-stick frying pan, place the chickens, skin side down, and cook over low heat. When the fat renders, and the skin turns golden brown and crispy, turn them over and cook the other side until thoroughly cooked.

3.   Take the chicken out of the pan. Remove the remaining oil from the frying pan using kitchen paper and add all the ingredients of the *teriyaki* sauce. Heat over medium to high heat and put the chicken back into the frying pan. Glaze the chicken with the sauce quickly. Place lettuce onto a plate and transfer the chicken on or beside it. Pour the remaining sauce over it and arrange lemon or lime slices aside.

Teriyaki Chicken Burger with Avocado Paste

If you put *teriyaki* chicken and vegetables together in a bun, it becomes *teriyaki* chicken burger. In this recipe, the chicken is flavored with garlic and soy sauce.

Garlic is never used in traditional Japanese cooking, but is often used in modern Japanese recipes. Avocado paste gives a rich and fresh taste.

鶏の照り焼きバーガー

Ingredients (4 servings)
1/2 onion
7-10 oz (200-300g) chicken breasts
Salt and pepper
Olive oil
1/2 tablespoon fresh garlic, chopped finely
Teriyaki sauce
 2 tablespoons Japanese soy sauce
 2 tablespoons sake
 1 tablespoon sugar
Avocado paste
 1 avocado
 2 teaspoons mayonnaise
 Salt and pepper
4 buns
Butter or margarine
Lettuce, shredded
Tomato, sliced

Procedure

1. Slice the onion thinly and soak in water for 30 minutes to remove hotness. Drain in a sieve and dry with a clean cloth or kitchen paper. Slice the chicken breasts thinly at a steep angle to make wide slices, and cut into 1-2 inches (2.5-5cm) pieces. Lightly sprinkle with salt and pepper and leave for 10 minutes.

2. Pat the chicken with kitchen paper. Place olive oil and the chopped garlic in a frying pan and heat over low heat. When aroma is released, add the chicken and cook thoroughly over medium heat. Add all the ingredients of the *teriyaki* sauce and baste the chicken with it.

3. *To make avocado paste*: Cut the avocado in half, remove the seed and scoop the fresh avocado into a bowl. Mash with a fork, add mayonnaise, salt and pepper to taste and combine until smooth.

4. Cut the buns in half and spread the butter or margarine evenly on both insides. Place the shredded lettuce, tomato, chicken (2), avocado paste (3) and onion (1) on half of a bun and cover with the other one. Serve on a plate.

Seafood

Japanese people are traditionally fish eaters. There are many kinds of fish and many ways to cook them. The simplest way is, of course, *sashimi*, which is raw fish. The other methods are grilled (*yaki-zakana*), simmered (*ni-zakana*), fried (*tempura*, *karaage*, *furai* and *kuwayaki*), steamed (*mushi-zakana*), processed (*kamaboko*), seafood pot (*nabe*), etc. The following recipes use some of these methods.

Tuna *Sashimi* with Hot Olive Oil and Avocado

Sashimi is one of the simplest of Japanese dishes. In the kitchens of Japanese restaurants, the chief chef is the one who works in the section making *sashimi*. He is called an *ita-mae*, which means "a person standing in front of a cutting board." In very traditional Japanese restaurants, the kitchen is divided into several sections depending on their function. These are washing, managing, decorating, baking, simmering, supporting and cutting. Usually cooks begin work in the washing section and gradually move up within the hierarchy, learning how to manage and cook food in each section until they finally reach the cutting section where *sashimi* is produced. A cook who reaches the cutting section becomes a chef and is then called an *ita-mae* and is permitted to have his own restaurant.

It seems very easy to make *sashimi*, but it requires professional techniques and wisdom based on much experience to make it nicely and safely. The simpler the dish, the keener the eyes of the chef must be in order to judge high quality ingredients.

As many people are scared of eating raw fish, in this recipe very hot olive oil is poured over the raw fish slices. For safety reasons, only very fresh tuna, snapper and farmed salmon are recommended for *sashimi*. Avocado adds richness and gives a fruity savor to the tuna *sashimi*.

鮪とアボカドのオリーブオイル和え

Ingredients (4 servings)
Marinade sauce
- 2 tablespoons Japanese soy sauce
- 2 teaspoons sake
- 2 teaspoons sugar

7 oz (200g) beans
1 avocado
7 oz (200g) fresh raw tuna
2 tablespoons olive oil
Fresh garlic, chopped finely
Wasabi or tabasco (optional)

Procedure

1. *To make marinade sauce*: Combine the Japanese soy sauce, sake and sugar in a glass bowl. Microwave for a short time to dissolve the sugar and to evaporate the alcohol. If you like spicy food, add a bit of *wasabi* (Japanese horseradish) or a few drops of tabasco when the sauce has cooled down.

2. Parboil the beans in salted water, drain in a sieve and cut them into 1 inch (2.5cm) pieces. Cut the avocado in half, remove the seed and chop it into cubes. Put the green beans and avocado in a small bowl and add half of the marinade sauce (1). Combine them lightly.

3. Cut the tuna into 1/2 inch (1cm) square cubes. Put them in the rest of the marinade sauce (1) and combine them.

4. Place olive oil and chopped garlic in a frying pan, and heat over low. When the garlic turns golden brown and crispy, immediately pour the hot garlic oil over the tuna (3) and mix. Add the green beans and avocado mixture (2) and combine with the tuna. Serve in a large dish to share or in individual dishes.

Salmon Steak with Soy Favor

(*Sake-no-kuwayaki*)

Frying in oil is a good way to seal the *umami* contained within fish. In Japanese this style of cooking is called *tempura*, *kara-age*, *furai* or *kuwayaki*. *Tempura*, *karaage* and *furai* are the names given to deep frying but *kuwayaki* means to dust with flour or potato starch and then to sauté in a frying pan. This *kuwayaki* salmon is a salmon steak with a Japanese taste.

鮭のくわ焼

Ingredients (4 servings)
4 fresh salmon fillets
Flour for dusting
Vegetable oil
Sauce
    1 tablespoon sake
    1 tablespoon Japanese soy sauce
    1/3 cup water (80ml) water
Thyme for preference
1 inch (2.5cm) square butter
Wedges of lemon or lime to taste

Procedure

1. Dry the salmon fillets with kitchen paper and dust with flour.

2. Heat vegetable oil in a frying pan and cook the fillets, skin-side down, until golden brown and crisp. Turn them over and cook the other sides. When they turn lightly brown, take them out of the pan and set aside.

3. Remove the oil left in frying pan with kitchen paper, add the sake, Japanese soy sauce and water and heat over high. Once it comes to a boil, add the thyme for preference, the salmon (2) and butter. Baste the salmon with the sauce.

4. Place lemon or lime wedges on serving plates and arrange the salmon on it. Top with thyme optionally.

Jack mackerel grilled under a grill.

Grilled Fish (*Yaki-zakana*)

In the past, this style of cooking, *yaki-zakana*, was done in every home. Fresh fish was roasted over charcoal fires outside the house. Nowadays fish is grilled on a grill and the smell is removed by an extractor fan. However the taste of *yaki-zakana* that has been roasted over a fire is far superior to that cooked on a grill. This is because at home it is difficult to grill fish under ideal conditions such as the high heat and distance from the flame.

This cooking method is however very easy – simply sprinkle salt over the fish and grill or cook in a frying pan. You can enjoy the different tastes given by different types of fish.

Ingredients (4 servings)
Fresh whole fish
    (snapper, bream, John Dory, mackerel, garfish, leather jacket, yellow tail, Pacific saury and so on)
Salt
Lemon or lime wedges

Procedure

1.   Scale the fish on both sides with the blunt edged of the knife, slit the belly, gut and clean the fish. Wash well under running cold water and dry with a kitchen towel or paper. Score the skin of the fish diagonally in a couple of places.

2.   Sprinkle salt evenly on each side and leave in the refrigerator for 1 hour for snapper, bream and John dory, 20-30 minutes for mackerel, garfish and leather jacket, and a couple of minutes for yellow tail and Pacific saury. Put a lot of salt inside the belly and on the tail to prevent burning.

3.   Oil the grill to prevent the skin from sticking. Place the fish under the hot grill or on the BBQ grill and cook. If you have neither of these, place a small amount of vegetable oil in a non-stick frying pan and cook fish on both sides over low to medium heat until golden brown. To cook thoroughly, cover with the lid during the last few minutes of cooking.

4.   Arrange on a serving plate with lemon or lime wedges.

Snapper cooked in a frying pan.

Simmered Squid
(*Ika-no-nimono*)

Squid is a sea creature known as devilfish. Its strange shape and slimy feel may have led Westerners to name it after the devil. While horrible to look at, squid is extremely rich in *umami*, and although it is often eaten as *sashimi*, cooked squid is also very good. But please note that if you heat it in a microwave, it will explode!

いかの煮物

Ingredients (4 servings)
18 oz (500g) skinned fresh squid, 2-3 squids
1 tablespoon Japanese soy sauce
1 tablespoon sake
1 tablespoon sugar
1/5 cup (50ml) water

Procedure

1. *To clean the squid*: Remove the guts and legs from the body and wash under running cold water. Cut the guts off the legs and discard them. Separate the legs by cutting off the bottom and cut the body into 1/2 inch (1cm) thick rings.

2. Place the squid in a pan and add all the remaining ingredients. Simmer over low to medium heat, stirring from time to time, until the liquid is reduced to less than half (about 10 minutes). Serve in a dish.

Simmered Fish

(*Ni-zakana*)

This is a very traditional dish, which in the past was cooked in every Japanese home. Unfortunately, with the national tendency to prefer meat to fish, its preparation at home is becoming rarer. However reports show that, as well as the nutritional value, fish has medical value, because of its EPA (eicosapentaenoic acid) and DHA (docosahexaenoic acid) content. These work to prevent vascular illnesses such as stroke and cardiac disease. So it may be worth eating more fish, especially seasonal varieties with an abundance of EPA and DHA. *Ni-zakana* is available with various types of fish.

Ingredients (2 servings)
Fish with bone and skin, 14 oz (400g) total
    (John Dory, flounder, red snapper, leather jacket, mackerel and so on)
Salt
Sauce
    1/5 cup (50ml) Japanese soy sauce
    1 cup (250ml) water
    2/5 cup (100ml) sake
    1 tablespoon sugar
    1 teaspoon ketchup
    Fresh ginger, sliced
2 green peppers cut lengthways

煮
魚

Procedure

1.   *To prepare the fish*: Scale the fish on both sides with the blunt edge of a knife, slit the belly and remove entrails. Wash well under running cold water. Cut larger sizes of fish into two or three pieces. Score the skin of the fish diagonally in a couple of places to help the sauce penetrate the fish.

2.   Cover the fish with a lot of salt and leave for 10 minutes to let the fishy liquid out of the body. Rinse the fish in a bowl of water, and set aside. Prepare ice water in a large bowl. Bring a pan of water to a boil and turn off the heat. Put the fish in it and when the color of the surface changes slightly (but note that some kinds of fish do not change their color) immediately plunge into the ice water to prevent overheating. Remove any remaining scales and debris, and change the water.

3.   Place a greaseproof paper on the bottom of the pan to prevent the skin from sticking to the bottom and distribute the fish (2) evenly on it. Add all the ingredients of the sauce, cover with a drop lid of foil or greaseproof paper and cook over medium heat for 10 minutes, pouring the sauce over the fish from time to time.

4.   Add the green pepper at the last minute of cooking. Turn off the heat, take out the green pepper and set aside. Let the fish stand for 10 minutes, covering them to cook with the remaining heat. Arrange the fish, green pepper and slices of ginger in individual dishes and pour the sauce over them.

Miso-flavored Mackerel

(*Saba-no-misoni*)

Combining peanut butter and fish may be a horrible thought for you, but a combination of peanut butter and soy sauce can be a substitute for *miso* in this dish.

Dark-fleshed fish smell fishier than white-fleshed fish in general. To erase the odor and to enhance the flavor, ginger, peanut butter and soy sauce work well as ingredients for sauce. If fresh mackerel is not available, try other fish such as bream or herring.

鯖のみそ煮

Ingredients (2 servings)
1 green pepper
2 mackerel fillets with skin, each about 5 oz (140g)
Salt
Sauce
    1 cup (240ml) water
    1/2 cup (120ml) sake
    1 tablespoon sugar
    1 tablespoon peanut butter
    1 1/2 tablespoons Japanese soy sauce
    1 teaspoon ketchup
A small clove of ginger, sliced thinly

Procedure

1. Cut green pepper lengthways. Cut each of the mackerel fillets into 2 pieces.

2. Cover the fish with a lot of salt and leave for 10 minutes. Prepare a bowl of ice water. Bring the water to a boil in a pan turn off the heat and blanch the fillets. When the color of the surface changes slightly, immediately plunge them into the ice water, clean off the debris in the water, and change the water a couple of times. This process is necessary to erase the fishy odor and to seal the *umami* in the fish.

3. Combine all the ingredients of the sauce in a large bottomed skillet and dissolve the peanut butter as much as you can. Place the mackerel and slices of ginger. Simmer over medium heat until the liquid is reduced to less than half. Add green pepper to one side of the skillet and cook for half to one minute. Transfer them to the serving dish and pour the sauce over them. Top with the ginger slices.

Stir-fried Prawns

(Ebi-no-kara-age)

In ancient times, Japanese culture was strongly influenced by China. The same is true for Japanese food culture. Soy sauce, soy products such as tofu, the eating of rice as a staple and the use of chopsticks, to name but a few practices, all originated in China. Over the years these gradually changed to Japanese tastes. But strangely, this was not the case for the Chinese custom of consuming a lot of oil. In this regard the two cultures diverged, moving in opposite directions. It was rare to use a lot of oil in very traditional Japanese cooking except in special dishes such as *tempura*, which was derived from the Spanish or Portuguese fritter. But oil has the power to improve the taste of food and to whet the appetite in spite of having no specific taste of its own. In this recipe, the *umami* in the prawns is sealed within by lightly dusting them unshelled in flour and then frying them in oil. Seasoning them with garlic and soy sauce may whet your appetite even more.

海老のから揚げ

Ingredients (2 servings)
10 1/2 oz (300g) prawns
Marinade
    1 tablespoon sake
    1 tablespoon Japanese soy sauce
    1 tablespoon ketchup
    1 teaspoon grated garlic
    1 teaspoon sugar
Flour
3 tablespoons vegetable oil

Procedure

1. Rinse the prawns briefly in cold water. Remove the heads of the prawns by hand. Cut off the tails and legs and split each prawn through the shell using scissors. Pull the dark veins out and then dry the prawns with a clean cloth or kitchen paper.

2. Combine all the ingredients of the marinade, and marinate the prawns (1) in it for at least 30 minutes.

3. Remove from the marinade and dust the prawns roughly with flour. Heat the oil in a wok over medium to high, and fry them quickly.

4. Drain excess oil and transfer them onto a serving dish.

Fried Salmon Marinated in Soy Sauce and Vinegar (*Nanban-zuke*)

The origin of this dish is "*escabeche de carapau*," which is Portuguese. It is said that the Portuguese were the first western people to visit Japan. In the 15th century they were known as "*nanban jin*" and it is said that this dish was introduced by them. The olive oil and garlic used in the original *escabeche* were replaced by soy sauce in the process to adjust to Japanese food culture. Vinegar was used as a preservative for the cooked fish at the time because there was no refrigeration.

鮭の南蛮漬け

Ingredients (4 servings)
Marinade
    2 medium onions
    1 red chili pepper
    1/5 cup (50ml) Japanese soy sauce
    3 tablespoons sugar
    2/5 cup (100ml) rice or apple vinegar
    4/5 cup (200ml) water
14 oz (400g) salmon fillets, bones removed.
Flour
Vegetable oil
1 medium carrot
1 continental or 2 Lebanese cucumbers
1/2 teaspoon salt

Procedure

1. *To make a marinade*: Slice the onion and cut the red chili pepper using scissors, both thinly. Place them in a large glass or stainless container, add the Japanese soy sauce and sugar, and mix. Let it stand for at least 10 minutes. When the onion softens, add the vinegar and water.

2. Cut the salmon meat into around 1 inch (2.5cm) squares. Dust them with flour and deeply fry with vegetable oil. When cooked, drain the oil with kitchen paper instantly, and immediately transfer them into the marinade (1) while they are very hot.

3. Cut the carrot and cucumber into thin 1-2 inches (2.5-5cm) julienne strips. Put them in a bowl, sprinkle the salt over them, mix and leave for 5 to 10 minutes. When liquid comes out of them, squeeze by hand to get rid of the liquid. Add them to the marinade (2), mix lightly and leave in refrigerator until serving.

Fish Cakes
(*Satsuma-age*)

Over the course of Japan's long history, during which the fishing industry was so important to people's lives, a great deal of knowledge and many techniques have been developed for processing seafood.

Making fish cakes called *kamaboko* is one such process and these do not require very fresh fish as is the case for *sashimi*. They are generally made by mincing the fish, then adding salt and seasonings before steaming or frying. Imitation crab, first developed in Japan but now available worldwide, may be the most famous ingredient in fish cakes.

It is quite troublesome to process fish at home so people now usually buy commercial fish cakes from a shop or supermarket. There are also many recipes specific to a particular area. *Satsuma-age* is a fish cake that was originally made in the southern area of Japan known as *Satsuma*. This is a simple recipe for making fish cakes at home and requiring no specifically Japanese ingredients except for Japanese soy sauce and sake.

Ingredients (4 servings)
Vegetable oil
1/2 onion, finely chopped
1/2 medium carrot, finely chopped
2 oz (60g) green beans, finely chopped
14 oz (400g) in total, fish fillets with white flesh (cod, snapper, sea bream, leather jacket and etc) and prawns, scallops ligaments and/or squid.
1/2 teaspoon salt
1 tablespoon sugar
1 tablespoon sake
1 tablespoon Japanese soy sauce
1 tablespoon peanut butter
1 egg
2 tablespoons potato starch or cornstarch
1 tablespoon fresh ginger finely chopped or other herbs for preference
Mayonnaise

さつま揚げ

Procedure
1.   Heat vegetable oil in a frying pan and sauté the onion until translucent. Add the carrot and green beans, sauté for a short time and then transfer to a large bowl.
2.   Remove the skin and bones from the fish fillets and cut roughly. Place all of the seafood in a food processor and add salt. Process until thickened. Then add the sugar, sake, Japanese soy sauce, peanut butter, egg and starch, and process again until well combined. Transfer it into the bowl of the vegetables (1) and add the ginger or other herbs for preference. Mix together with a spoon or spatular until evenly incorporated.
3.   Preheat ample vegetable oil to 340 F (170 C) in a wok or a frying pan. Shape into small patties, patting on both sides with hands, and slip one by one into the oil. Deeply fry until golden brown. Drain the excess oil and serve on a plate. Set aside mayonnaise as a dip.

Meat

Miso-flavored Pork
(Buta-no-miso-zuke)

Miso is a very important seasoning in Japanese cooking. This savory paste is made from fermented soybeans and salt. In old days, *miso* used to be homemade and so the taste differed depending on the recipe used in each home. But now *miso* is made commercially and you can find various types in the shops. Japanese people have *miso* soup with rice every day and so take in soy protein because of this. However *miso* is not only a soup, it is a favorite seasoning in many recipes. This is one such dish. Since it can be difficult to find good *miso* outside Japan, this recipe combines peanut butter and soy sauce. Therefore the nutritious component of this sauce is of course different from the original *miso*, but the flavor and taste of cooked pork are exactly the same as pork marinated in *miso* sauce.

豚のみそ漬け

Ingredients (2 servings)
Marinating sauce
    2 tablespoons sake
    1 tablespoon sugar
    1 tablespoon peanut butter
    2 tablespoons Japanese soy sauce
14 oz (400g) thick-cut pork chucks (about 1/2 inch (1cm) thick)
Green salad

Procedure

1.   Combine all the ingredients of the marinating sauce and dissolve the peanut butter, stirring with a spoon as much as you can.

2.   Put the marinade (1) and the pork in a zip-lock bag. Remove the air and cover the meat slices with the sauce. Close the bag and keep in the refrigerator overnight or even for two nights.

3.   Take the pork out of the zip-lock bag and remove the marinade sauce from the surface of the pork using kitchen paper. Brush the grid with vegetable oil and grill the pork under a griller or on a BBQ grill, or bake in an oven at 450 F (230 C). If you have neither of these, heat vegetable oil in a frying pan and cook on the both sides. Cut into bite-sized pieces on a cutting board and serve on a plate with green salad.

Gingered Pork

(Buta-no-shouga-yaki)

This is very popular dish for Japanese home cooking. Thinly sliced meat is cooked and eaten quickly. The ginger and apple included in the sauce tenderize the meat. This dish is best served with plain rice.

豚のしょうが焼き

Ingredients (4 servings)
Ginger sauce
    2 tablespoons sake
    2 tablespoons Japanese soy sauce
    1 teaspoon sugar
    2 teaspoons finely chopped or ground ginger
    3 tablespoons grated apple or apple juice
14 oz (400g) pork chuck, loin, or thigh, thinly sliced
Flour
Vegetable oil
Green salad

Procedure
1. Combine all the ingredients of the ginger sauce.
2. Lightly dust the pork slices with flour. Heat the vegetable oil in a frying pan and fry both sides of the pork slices over medium heat. When cooked, take them out of the pan and set aside.
3. Remove the extra oil left in the pan using kitchen paper, add the ginger sauce (1) and bring to a simmer. Bring back the pork (2) into the pan and baste with the sauce. Serve with green salad on a dish. Accompany with plain rice if desired.

Sukiyaki Beef with Rice (*Gyu don*)

Sukiyaki is one of Japan's most famous dishes. About 150 years ago, when the common people in Japan were permitted to eat beef for the first time, they had no idea how to prepare it. A restaurant which provided beef dishes opened in *Yokohama* city and there the beef was thinly sliced like *sashimi*. It was cooked with Japanese soy sauce, sugar and sake and vegetables such as Japanese leeks. This seems to have been the beginning of *sukiyaki*, which became a very popular dish with the common people and later became famous throughout the world. If you serve *sukiyaki* beef with plain rice, it becomes a dish called *gyu-don*.

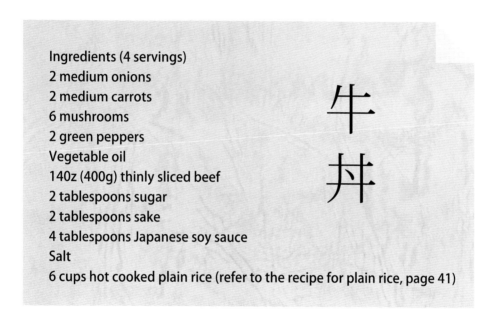

Ingredients (4 servings)
2 medium onions
2 medium carrots
6 mushrooms
2 green peppers
Vegetable oil
14oz (400g) thinly sliced beef
2 tablespoons sugar
2 tablespoons sake
4 tablespoons Japanese soy sauce
Salt
6 cups hot cooked plain rice (refer to the recipe for plain rice, page 41)

Procedure

1.   Slice the onions into wedges. Cut the carrots in half lengthways and slice thinly. Clean the mushrooms and cut into bite-sized pieces. Slice the green pepper lengthways.

2.   Place the vegetable oil in a large bottomed saucepan and heat over a medium heat. Add the beef and sugar, and sauté. When the beef is half cooked, add the sake, Japanese soy sauce and all of the vegetables (1) except for green pepper and then simmer.

3.   When simmered, add the green pepper and cook until it turns bright green. Sprinkle salt to taste. Place the plain rice in a dish and put the *sukiyaki* beef and soup beside or over it.

Beef and Vegetable Pot

(Shabu-Shabu)

Thinly sliced meat makes it easy for Japanese people to eat meat with chopsticks.

The slices of meat used in *shabu-shabu* are extraordinarily thin, like paper. As it is very hard to slice a joint into such thin slices, half frozen meat sliced by machines is usually purchased from stores. The way of eating *shabu-shabu* is similar to the way cheese fondue which is eaten in Switzerland. In *shabu-shabu*, thinly sliced meat is cooked at the table in the same way as the Swiss cook the cheese and bread in a fondue.

Shabu-shabu has nutritional merits in that this method reduces the intake of fat from the meat and a large amount of vegetables are cooked by plunging them into boiling water. Seasoning is provided by dipping the cooked meat and vegetables into a favorite sauce just before eating. In Japan, a sesame sauce and a combination sauce of soy sauce and citrus called *ponzu* are popularly flavored as dips. Here sesame sauce is replaced by a peanut butter sauce. If you have your own favorites such as tomato sauce, Mexican salsa sauce or whatever, you can use them instead.

Although *shabu-shabu* is one way of cooking Japanese style, it also provides a new way to enjoy a meal with all the members of a family at the same table. Cooking and eating together gives us an opportunity to talk with each other, for children to learn how to cook, to feel happy just being together and so on. Enjoy cooking and eating together with your family or friends.

Ingredients (4 servings)

Sauces for dipping

A: Citrus-shabu-shabu sauce

   4 tablespoons Japanese soy sauce

   1 tablespoon sugar

   1 tablespoon lemon or lime juice

   2 tablespoons orange juice

B: Peanut butter shabu-shabu sauce

   1 tablespoon peanut butter

   1 tablespoon sugar

   1 tablespoon Japanese soy sauce

   1 tablespoon rice or apple vinegar or lemon juice

   1 tablespoon orange juice

Vegetables

   Carrots

   Oyster mushrooms

   Spring onions

   Zucchini

   Chinese cabbage

14-20 oz (400-600g) very thinly sliced beef

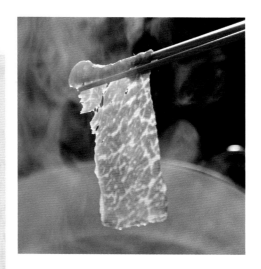

しゃぶしゃぶ

Procedure

1. *To make sauce for dipping;*

A: *Citrus shabu-shabu sauce*: Combine all the ingredients and dissolve the sugar.

B: *Peanut butter shabu-shabu sauce*: Combine all of the ingredients and stir until smooth.

Divide the sauce by pouring equal amounts into individual bowls.

2. Cut each vegetable into bite-sized pieces, Trim stems from the oyster mushrooms and tear into small clusters. Arrange each kind of vegetable separately along with the beef on a large plate. .

3. Set a portable gas or electric heater on a table. Put water into a large casserole and heat on the portable heater over high heat. Let everyone hold their own bowls of dipping sauce. Since the high temperature makes the meat tough, when the water is heated to around 175 F (80 C), add the beef slice by slice using chopsticks. When cooked, immediately transfer to the dipping sauces and eat. But for the first time, dip only the tip of the meat slice, because the sauce is made thick allowing for the fact that it will be gradually diluted with the cooking water.

4. Skim any scum off the surface and add the vegetables. When cooked, dip in the dipping sauces and eat. If the water is reduced, add more water, and when the dip is diluted, add more dip to the individual bowls. Each member can take whatever they like from the platters of meat and vegetables, cook it, dip it, and eat.

Teriyaki Hamburger Steak

Hamburgers are now a very popular food throughout the world. They originated as a food for laborers in Hamburg, Germany in the 13th century. From here they spread all over the world due to the availability of various types of meat, the convenience for children and the elderly, who find it difficult to chew tough meat, and the ability to change the flavor by adding seasoning. At the end of World War II, hamburger steak made of minced meat, which was cheaper than steaks, provided an important source of protein for people in Japan. Furthermore, the fact that hamburger steaks could be eaten using chopsticks as *okazu* for the staple food, rice, unlike tough steaks, made hamburger steak one of the Japan's national favorites. This is still a very popular Japanese dish today.

照り焼きハンバーグ

Ingredients (4 servings)
Salad
  1/2 head cabbage, remove the center core
  Lettuce
  Tomatoes
Hamburger patties
  18 oz (500g) minced meat (beef and/or pork)
  1 teaspoon salt
  Pepper and nutmeg
  1 medium onion, finely chopped
  3/5 cup (150ml) breadcrumbs
  1 egg
Vegetable oil
Teriyaki sauce
  3 tablespoons Japanese soy sauce
  3 tablespoons sake
  3 tablespoons water
  1 tablespoon sugar
10 oz (280g) mushrooms, thinly sliced
Some oyster mushrooms (optional)

Procedure

1. *To make salad*: Shred the cabbage leaves finely and tear the lettuce into bite-sized pieces by hand. If the tomatoes are big, cut into bite-sized pieces.

2. *To make hamburger patties*: Place the meat, salt, pepper, nutmeg, chopped onion, breadcrumbs and egg in a medium bowl. Mix well using your hand until sticky. Divide the mixture into eight and shape into round or oval patties patting lightly on both sides.

3. Heat vegetable oil in a frying pan over medium heat and cook the patties (2). When both sides are browned, pour in all the ingredients of *teriyaki* sauce, mushrooms and oyster mushrooms. Heat over medium heat turning the patties over from time to time. When the patties are cooked through, take them out of the pan and set aside. Heat the sauce until your desired thickness and then put the hamburger steaks back into the pan to heat.

4. Place the salad (1) on individual plates and put the hamburger patties (3) on the side. Pour the mushrooms and the sauce over the patties and serve.

Simmered Pork (*Yaki-buta*) and Mashed Potatoes

焼き豚

In *Okinawa*, one of the southern islands of Japan, there is a traditional way of cooking a side of pork, which is called *yakibuta*. Pork belly is commonly used in this dish because it becomes soft when cooked and the fat has *umami*. First the pork is boiled in a large pan of water and then left overnight in a cold place. The next day the solidified fat on the surface of the water is removed. The meat is then cooked with soy sauce and the other ingredients. It is sliced into pieces and served with plain rice as *okazu*.

It is commonly known that the people living in these islands have a longer lifespan than people living in other parts of Japan. The scientific reason for this is unclear, but the relaxing atmosphere and the unique food culture are considered to be part of the reasons.

Here, instead of pork belly, chuck, loin or dark meat, which has less fat, is used in order to make cooking easier and simmered in English tea. Mashed potatoes are served as a side dish instead of plain rice.

Ingredients (2 servings)

Yaki-buta
- 18 oz (500g) pork, chuck, loin or dark meat
- Vegetable oil
- Water
- 1 teabag, without string
- 1 1/2 tablespoons sugar
- 1/4 cup (60ml) sake
- 1/4 cup (60ml) Japanese soy sauce
- 1 leek, cleaned
- 2/3-1 oz (20-30g) fresh ginger, cut into a couple of pieces
- 1 tablespoon of rice or apple vinegar

Mashed potato
- 3 medium-sized potatoes
- Water
- 1-teaspoon salt
- 1 cup (240ml) milk
- Butter

Side vegetables
- Carrots and any green vegetables (Asparagus, broccoli, green beans, peas, etc.)
- Salt
- Butter

Procedure

Yaki-buta

1. Tie the hunk of pork with a string so that the hunk does not break up even after long simmering and the *umami* is sealed inside. Heat the vegetable oil in a frying pan and brown each side of pork over medium to high heat. When browned, transfer into a thick-bottomed deep pan and add water until the pork is completely immersed. Then add one teabag, sugar, sake, Japanese soy sauce, leek and ginger for seasoning and flavoring. Remove any scum from the surface and cover with a lid. Simmer over low heat for one hour.

2. Add the vinegar at the end of simmering to make the taste rich and heat for ten more minutes. Remove from heat and let it stand unopened until cooled down to room temperature, because the taste of the liquid goes into the meat while it slowly cools down.

3. Take the pork out of the pot, drain the sauce in a sieve to remove the ginger, leek and debris, and place the sauce in the other pot. Simmer the sauce uncovered until reduced to less than half. Take the string off the pork and leave in sauce just before serving.

Mashed potatoes

1. Peel the potatoes and cut into quarters. Soak in water for a while to remove excess starch.

2. Drain the potatoes in a sieve, place in a pot and add water until completely immersed. Add the salt and cook thoroughly over medium heat.

3. Drain in a sieve, return to the pot and mash while the potatoes are hot. Add milk and butter, and heat again, stirring with a wooden spoon until thickened.

Side vegetables

1. Cut each vegetable into bite-sized pieces.

2. Place water and a pinch of salt in a pan. Add the carrots and cook over high heat. When pierced with a skewer, add the green vegetables, parboil, and drain together in a sieve.

3. Return each vegetable to the pan, add butter and toss them to season with butter.

Heat the pot of the pork over high heat. When heated, take the pork out of the liquid and slice into 1/2 inch (1 cm) thickness. Transfer onto a plate and pour the sauce over the meat. Serve with mashed potatoes and side vegetables.

Spring Rolls *(Harumaki)*

Spring rolls are a very popular Chinese food worldwide and so too in Japan. Although their preparation appears complicated, the process is actually quite simple. Prepare your favorite stuffing and seal this in Chinese pastry, then deep fry until golden brown. The ingredients can be anything you choose such as meat, seafood, vegetables, etc. but it is essential to cook these before placing them inside the pastry. The tasty liquid that escapes from the ingredients is thickened with the starch liquid added at the end and it remains inside the pastry case. So the *umami* from the liquid will spread in the mouth immediately once you bite into the crispy skin.

Ingredients (4 servings)

Starch mixture for gelling

    2 tablespoons potato starch or cornstarch + 4 tablespoons water

Stuffing

    Vegetable oil

    10 oz (280g) minced meat (pork, beef or chicken)

    1 medium carrot, chopped into small pieces

    1 large cabbage leave, chopped finely

    4 mushrooms, chopped into small pieces

    1 teaspoon fresh ginger, finely chopped

    1 tablespoon leek, white part only, or shallot or onion, chopped finely

    2 1/2 tablespoons Japanese soy sauce

    2 tablespoons sake

    1 teaspoon sugar

    Pepper

    Sesame oil

Flour mixture for glue

    1 tablespoon flour + 1 tablespoon water

10 to 12 spring roll sheets

春巻き

Procedure

1. *To make starch mixture for gelling*: mix the potato starch or cornstarch and water at 1:2 ratio (v/v) in a cup and leave.

2. Heat vegetable oil in a frying pan and fry the minced meat over high heat until brown. Add all the vegetables to the meat and fry them together. Season with Japanese soy sauce, sake, sugar and pepper. Stir the starch mixture (1) well with a spoon and add it slowly to the mixture of meat and vegetables while stirring. Heat at least for 90 seconds to thicken and add the sesame oil for flavoring. Remove from the heat, spread on a tray and divide into 10 to 12 sections.

3. *To make flour mixture for glue*: Combine the flour and water, and mix.

4. Spread a spring roll sheet on a flat board. Place one section of the stuffing (2) on it and wrap. Close the end with the glue made of flour mixture (3). Repeat the same action with the rest of the stuffing.

5. Heat ample vegetable oil in a wok or frying pan and fry the spring rolls closing side down over low to medium heat. Turn them over, frying both sides evenly to golden brown. Drain the excess oil with kitchen paper and serve on a plate.

Gyouza modoki Pasties

Pasty is a Westerner's favorite food. Japanese recipes similar to western pasties include dumplings called *gyouza*, *shumai*, *nikuman*, meat and potato croquettes and minced meat cutlets. These are all very popular home-cooked foods in Japan. Japanese people really love those dishes. *Umami* from meat and vegetables is enclosed in small shaped dumplings or deep fried batter. In this recipe, meat and cabbage, the ingredients of *gyouza*, are used as the stuffing. The texture of fresh cabbage in a pasty may be new to you. Commercial pie pastry is used in this recipe to save the work required to make it at home.

餃子風ミートパイ

Ingredients (6 servings)
1 large onion, chopped finely
1/4 cabbage, cut into 1/2 inch (1cm) square pieces
Butter
18 oz (500g) minced meat (pork or beef)
1 teaspoon salt
Pepper and nutmeg
Commercial pie pastry, thawed
Ketchup

Procedure
1. Place butter in a frying pan, sauté the onion over low heat until translucent and a little brown, and then let it cool.
2. Place the minced meat in a bowl, add salt, pepper and nutmeg, and knead well until sticky. Add the onion (1) and cabbage, and mix by hand.
3. Roll out the pasty on a lightly floured surface and extend to 1.2 to 1.5 times its area. Cut out into 15cm diameter circles using the edge of a bowl. Place spoonfuls of the filling (2) on one half of each pasty circle and fold the plain half of the pastry over the filling. Seal the edges by crimping with the prongs of a fork. Make a couple of breaks on top by using a knife.
4. Preheat the oven to 350 F (180 C). Place the turnovers (3) on a baking sheet and bake in the oven for 15 to 20 minutes. Confirm that the meat is cooked thoroughly by piercing with a skewer and then serve with ketchup.

Vegetables

Here are some traditional ways of cooking vegetables at home in Japan:

- *Nimono* – vegetables simmered with *dashi* (extract from dried bonito flakes and dried *konbu*), soy sauce, *mirin* (sweetened sake) and sugar.
- *Kimpira* – vegetables cut thinly, stir-fried and seasoned mainly with soy sauce and *mirin*.
- *Ohitashi* – vegetables parboiled and seasoned mainly with *dashi*.
- *Aemono* – vegetables dressed by other ingredients such as tofu, seafood, beans, fruits, nuts and etc.
- *Tsukemono* – vegetables fermented or salted for preservation. They are fermented in rice bran or malted rice, or placed in soy sauce, *miso* and so on. There are many kinds of *tsukemono* in different local areas.
- *Sunomono* – vegetables with the liquid squeezed out and seasoned with vinegar and sugar or *mirin*.
- *Tempura* – vegetables dipped in batter and deep-fried.
- *Itamemono* –stir fried vegetables
Nowadays, salads made of fresh vegetables have become very popular. Here, the recipes for *nimono*, *kimpira*, *ohitashi*, *tsukemono*, *tempura* and Japanese style salads are shown.

Japanese Salad
(*Asa-zuke*)
(vegetarian dish)

Nutritionally we need a lot of fresh vegetables and fruit for good health. But we cannot eat the amounts of fresh salad needed at each meal. Vegetables contain lots of water, which makes them bulky. In Japanese cooking, salt is often used to reduce the water as plant cells shrink when sprinkled with salt (plasmolysis) and the water within is reduced. This allows people to take in a lot of raw, fresh vegetables.

For example, in instant *tsukemono* the volume of salad is reduced by salt and herbs such as ginger and Japanese basil, called *shiso*, and some kinds of citrus fruits are often added for flavor instead of salad dressings. The simplest way of cooking is often the best way to enjoy the real taste of fresh food.

Ingredients (4 servings)

18 oz (500g) vegetables in all

    Carrots, peeled

    Continental or Lebanese cucumbers, and/or zucchini

    Cabbage soft leaves without center core

1 tablespoon salt

1 tablespoon sugar

1 tablespoon rice or apple vinegar

1-2 tablespoons fresh ginger or lemon zest, finely slivered

1 teaspoon Japanese soy sauce (optional)

1 to 2 tablespoons sesame oil (optional)

浅漬け

Procedure

1. Cut the carrots into 1-inch (2.5cm) thin julienne strips. Slice the cucumber thinly. Chop the cabbage leaves into bite-sized pieces. If the cabbage leaves are thick, slice into thin pieces.

2. Place all the vegetables (1) in a large bowl, and sprinkle the salt and sugar. Mix them together and leave for 5 minutes. When they begin to soften, mix again and leave for a further 15 minutes.

3. Squeeze out the liquid that comes out of the vegetables using both hands, add the vinegar, slivered ginger or lemon zest and mix. Optionally drizzle with Japanese soy sauce and/or sesame oil to add flavor. Serve in a dish.

Green Beans Dressed with Peanuts and Soy

(*Ingen-no-aemono*) (vegetarian dish)

In comparison to the vegetables as a side dish in Western cuisine, Japanese *ohitashi* and *aemono* are cooked for a short time in order to retain the freshness of the vegetables. They are parboiled for a short period and seasoned or dressed simply with other ingredients such as sesame seeds, citrus, bonito flakes, ginger and etc. Here, fresh green beans are combined with crushed peanuts instead of sesame seeds.

いんげんのピーナッツ和え

Ingredients (4 servings)
Unsalted roasted peanuts
7 oz (200g) green beans
4 cups (1L) water
1 teaspoon salt
1 teaspoon Japanese soy sauce
1/2 teaspoon sugar

Procedure

1.   Put the peanuts in a plastic bag and finely crush with a rolling pin. Cut off the ends of the green beans by hand.

2.   Bring a pan of the water to a boil and add the salt. Parboil the beans until tender but still crunchy. Drain the green beans in a sieve, cut into 1 inch (2.5 cm) pieces and put them in a medium bowl. Add the soy sauce, sugar and the crushed peanuts (1) and mix. Serve in a dish.

Stir-fried Vegetables (*Kimpira*) (vegetarian dish)

Kimpira means to cook vegetables in the Japanese style. In Japan *kimpira* is commonly made with burdock or lotus roots, but since these are not popular foods outside of Japan, carrots and potatoes are used here instead. Vegetables used in *kimpira* are usually cut into julienne strips or thinly sliced in order to make them easy to cook, season and hold with chopsticks and chew. With *kimpira* it is essential to retain the crispness of the raw vegetables by cooking them very lightly. Although vegetables in *kimpira* are usually seasoned with Japanese soy sauce and *mirin* (sweetened sake), any seasoning or herbs can be used instead.

人参のきんぴら

Carrot *Kimpira*

Ingredients (4 servings)
2 medium carrots, peeled
2 tablespoons vegetable oil
2 teaspoons peanut butter
1 tablespoon Japanese soy sauce
1 tablespoon rice, apple or wine vinegar
Crushed roast peanuts (refer to the recipe of
   Green Beans Dressed with Peanuts and Soy,
   page 131)

Procedure

1.   Cut the carrots into 2-inch (5cm) thin julienne strips.

2.   Heat the vegetable oil in a frying pan. Add the carrots and stir fry over a medium heat. When the carrots start to soften, add the peanut butter, Japanese soy sauce and vinegar and stir. Turn off the heat while the carrots are still crisp and serve. Sprinkle the crushed roast peanuts on top.

Potato *Kimpira*

Ingredients (4 servings)
4 medium sized potatoes, peeled
2 tablespoons olive oil
2oz (60g) sliced bacon
1 clove of garlic, chopped finely
1 red chili pepper, thinly sliced with seeds removed
Salt and pepper

Procedure

1.   Cut the potatoes into about 2 inch lengths (5 cm) of thin juliennes and soak in water for a couple of minutes to remove any excess starch. Drain in a sieve and dry with clean cloth or kitchen paper. Cut the slices of bacon roughly into smaller pieces.

2.   Heat the olive oil in a frying pan over low heat and then add the bacon. Once the fat has been released from the bacon, add the garlic and red chili pepper. Continue to heat until the aroma is released. Add the potatoes and stir fry over medium heat until the potatoes are cooked but still retain their crispness. Season with salt and pepper and serve.

Simmered Vegetables and Meat
(Nikujaga)

As much less *umami* is contained in vegetables than in meat or fish, we traditionally season the vegetables with *dashi* extracted from dried *konbu* (kelp seaweed) and *katsuo-bushi* (flakes of dried bonito). Simmering vegetables in a liquid containing *dashi*, soy sauce, *mirin* (sweetened sake) and/or sugar, causes the *umami*, saltiness and sweetness from the liquid to be absorbed by the vegetables. The vegetable dish made in this method is called *nimono*. Usually root vegetables such as radishes, carrots, burdock, lotus root, taros, etc. are used as ingredients because they do not break up during simmering.

In this recipe, because it is difficult to get dried *konbu* and *katsuo-bushi* outside of Japan, one of the *nimono* dishes called *nikujaga* in which meat is used as an *umami* ingredient is shown.

Ingredients (4 servings)

4 medium potatoes, peeled

2 medium carrots, peeled

7 oz (200g) green beans

Sauce

   3 tablespoons sake

   1 to 1 1/2 tablespoons sugar

   3 tablespoons Japanese soy sauce

   1/2 apple, ground

   1/2 cup (120ml) water

7oz (200g) beef or pork, thinly sliced and cut into bite-sized pieces

2 tablespoons vegetable oil

Procedure

1.   Cut each potato into quarters and soak in water to remove any excess starch. Cut the carrots into one or two bite-sized pieces. Remove the end of the green beans and cut into halves or thirds. Combine all of the ingredients of the sauce.

2.   Drain the potatoes in a sieve. Heat the vegetable oil in a large pan and sauté the meat. Add the sauce (1) to season the meat and then add the potatoes and carrots. Cover with a lid and simmer over low to medium heat tossing the pan from time to time in order to season all the ingredients evenly with the sauce. Add the green beans and cook for the last few minutes.

3.   When the potatoes are thoroughly cooked, remove from heat and leave for 10 minutes covered. Add salt to taste and arrange nicely in a large dish or individual dishes.

Pickles Japanese-style
(vegetarian dish)

Vegetables that are preserved in a liquid consisting of vinegar, salt, sugar, and some kinds of herbs are commonly called pickles. The acetic acid in vinegar plays a very important role in preserving vegetables for a long time. But unfortunately, Western pickles cannot be an *okazu* (side dish) with rice for Japanese people, because the taste does not complement plain rice. This recipe shows how Western pickles can be altered to give a more Japanese taste and how they can become a dish for *okazu*. Fresh Japanese soy sauce seems to be an indispensable ingredient in the process. Olive oil is added to reduce the sourness of the vinegar.

野菜のマリネ

Ingredients (10 servings)
Marinade sauce
- 2 medium onions
- 1-2 cloves of garlic
- A red or green chili pepper
- 1 teaspoon salt
- 2 tablespoons sugar
- 1/3 cup (80ml) soy sauce
- 4/5 cup (200ml) rice or apple vinegar
- 2/5 cup (100ml) olive oil

1kg (35 oz) vegetables in all
- Carrots
- Green beans
- Cauliflower
- Turnips
- Mushrooms
- Zucchini
- Celery

Procedure

1. *To make marinade sauce*: Slice the onions, garlic and chili pepper very thinly. Place them in a large glass or stainless bowl, add the salt, sugar and soy sauce and mix. Let it stand for at least 30 minutes until the onions soften. Add the vinegar and then drop in the olive oil little by little, stirring for emulsification.

2. Cut the carrots into one to two bite-sized pieces. Take off the ends of the green beans and cut in halves or thirds. Divide the cauliflower into small bunches. Cut the turnips and mushrooms in halves or quarters, and the zucchini into wedges. Cut the celery into bite-sized pieces.

3. Bring a large pot of water to a boil, add the carrots, green beans, cauliflowers, turnips, mushrooms, zucchini and celery by turns and parboil them. One to two minutes after coming to a boil, drain all the vegetables in a large sieve.

4. Immediately transfer them to the marinade sauce (1) while they are very hot and mix. Leave for at least 5 hours before serving.

*Note: Olive oil hardens when chilled. Microwaving for a short time is recommended before serving if hardened.

Pickled Ginger

(*Gari*)(vegetarian dish)

Ginger products such as ginger snaps, ginger ale, ginger tea, ginger candy, etc. are popular foods in Western countries. The aroma and spicy element whet our appetites. Ginger has also been used as a natural remedy in many countries, because it is considered effective in increasing the metabolism and warming the body.

In Japan, fresh grated ginger is used as a condiment, especially during the hot and humid summers. But it is also used in winter as a natural food remedy for colds. Japanese people really love this herbal root.

The most famous Japanese ginger product known worldwide may be pickled ginger, called *gari*, which is always served as a condiment at *sushi* restaurants. It is amazing that this pickle is internationally loved by many people, as *sushi* is too. It would be lovely to have the pickled ginger not only with *sushi* but also with other foods.

Ingredients (10 servings)
18 oz (500g) fresh ginger, peeled
Marinade
    1 3/4 cup (400ml) rice or apple vinegar
    7 oz (200g) sugar
    1 teaspoon salt

Procedure

1. Slice the ginger very thinly using a slicer or slice as thinly as possible using a knife and soak in water for one hour.

2. *To make marinade*: Place all the ingredients of the marinade in a glass jar and heat in a microwave to dissolve the sugar and reduce the acidity of the vinegar.

3. Drain the ginger slices (1) in a sieve. Bring a pot of water to a boil, plunge in them and simmer for three minutes over medium heat. Drain in a sieve and squeeze lightly to remove excess water using a clean cloth. While they are still hot, soak in the marinade (2) and leave at room temperature for a couple of hours. Preserve in refrigerator. The taste is better after one week.

Vegetable *Tempura*
(vegetarian dish)

Tempura is a famous Japanese food, but it was originally introduced to Japan from Spain or Portugal. Usually this deep-fried food is dipped in a sauce called *tsuyu* that is made of *dashi*, soy sauce and *mirin* in order to season and rinse the oil away when eating. But because it is difficult to get *dashi*, Japanese soy sauce diluted with water is used as a dip in this recipe. If you cannot even get Japanese soy sauce, salt alone would be fine as a seasoning.

野菜の天ぷら

Ingredients (4 servings)

4 oz (120g) string beans

1 medium carrot, peeled

1 zucchini

1/2 parsnip

Japanese soy dip-tsuyu

    2 tablespoons Japanese soy sauce

    6 tablespoons water

    1 teaspoon sugar

    Ginger, ground to taste (optional)

Tempura batter

    6 tablespoons flour, kept in refrigerator

    4 tablespoons ice water

Vegetable oil

Natural salt

Procedure

1. Halve the string beans lengthways and then cut those in half. Cut the carrot, zucchini and parsnip into 2 to 3-inch (5 to 7.5cm) thin julienne strips. Combine them in a bowl.

2. *To make Japanese soy dip-tsuyu*: Combine all the ingredients and microwave to dissolve the sugar in seconds. Add ground ginger if desired.

3. Place the vegetable oil deep enough for frying in a wok or heavy bottomed deep pot and start heating the oil to 355 F (180 C).

4. Place the chilled flour and ice water at 3:2 ratios (v/v) in a bowl and mix lightly so that gluten does not come out of the flour to make the *tempura* crispy. Add some of the mixture of vegetables (1), mix lightly, bind several pieces of vegetables together by hand, and slip slowly into heated oil (3). If they scatter, bind together using tongs. Fry for about 2 minutes and when the batter turns crisp, transfer onto a wired rack to drain the oil. Repeat the same action with the remaining vegetable mixture. If the batter runs short, add chilled flour and ice water at the same ratio. Serve on a paper placed on a plate with Japanese soy dip-*tsuyu* or natural salt.

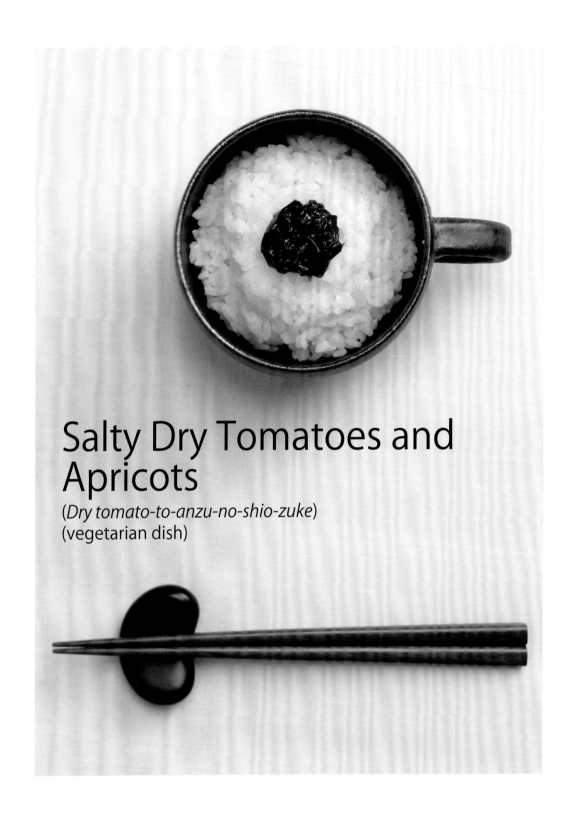

Salty Dry Tomatoes and Apricots

(Dry tomato-to-anzu-no-shio-zuke)
(vegetarian dish)

Umeboshi, which is salted plum, is a very traditional Japanese food. It is mainly eaten with plain rice and often buried in rice balls (see page 47), because the citric acid and strong salt contained in *umeboshi* work as natural preservatives for plain rice. This recipe may be especially for Japanese people who cannot get *umeboshi* overseas. The taste and flavor are not exactly the same as original *umeboshi*, but your desire for Japanese simple food may be realized by this alternative.

Ingredients (4 to 6 servings)
2/3oz (20g) dry tomatoes
2oz (60g) dry apricots
Water
1 teaspoons salt
2 tablespoons lemon juice

Procedure

1. Soak the dry tomatoes and dry apricots in water until completely immersed and leave overnight.

2. Place the tomatoes and apricots with the liquid (1) in food processor and process until finely chopped or ground. Transfer them in a pan and add the salt. Cook over low heat until the liquid evaporated and then remove from the heat. Add the lemon juice and mix. Serve with plain rice. Keep the leftover in refrigerator.

ドライトマトと杏子の塩漬け

Desserts

It is known that the oldest sweet mentioned in Japanese history was dry persimmons. In the old days, sugar was a very special food that was available only to a very limited number of nobles or wealthy people.

Around 150 years ago, Japan was opened to foreign nations and the use of sugar spread among the common Japanese people, but sugar was still expensive and considered a special food by the local population of Japan. The remarkable economic development after World War II suddenly made large amounts of affordable sugar available for consumption by the entire population. People were suddenly able to enjoy many kinds of western sweets such as cakes, candies, chocolates, cookies, ice creams and so on.

The consumption of sugar continued to increase along with the development of the Japanese economy, but interestingly the increase stopped during the 1960s. Currently, the consumption of sugar per person in Japan is the lowest amongst the developed countries of the world. Although westerners who visit or live in Japan often complain that Japanese sweets are not sweet, this is considered a Japanese natural habit. Japanese tongues cannot tolerate too much sweetness, because we eat a lot of carbohydrates and blood sugar increases enough due to this.

Traditional Japanese sweets are called *wa-gashi*, and are usually eaten at tea time. There are many kinds, including *anko*, which is made from *azuki* beans and sugar. *Anko* originated in China, but Chinese *anko* is not sweet. It may have gradually become a Japanese sweet over a long period of time. *Wa-gashi* are nice to have with green tea, but unfortunately in most cases, they are not very attractive sweets for Westerners because of the beans' smell and texture.

Other sweets such as cakes, cookies, chocolate, ice cream, etc. are called *yoh-gashi*. *Yoh* means western and *gashi* means sweets. So *yoh-gashi* means sweets that have originated in Western countries. In traditional Japan, no custom existed for the baking of cakes and sweets at home. These were goods to buy at shops. Now, however, home baking has become very popular due to the introduction of ovens as popular kitchen appliances. However many pastry shops still do good business in Japan.

Because of the reasons given above, it is very difficult to find a recipe for Japanese sweets that can be said to be internationally loved.

Traditionally Japanese people drink green tea after meals and say "*gochi-so-sama*" which means "thank you for this meal" as a way to end the meal. This allows us to feel that the meal is at an end. A cup of bitter green tea after a meal is not just a cup of tea. It is intended to distinguish the time and space of a meal from other time and space. So even during routine meals food is always treated with reverence. Furthermore, it has been shown that catechin, which is contained in abundance in green tea, has an anticancer effect. So having a cup of green tea after every meal may provide additional medicinal benefits to the drinkers.

In Japan, seasonal fresh fruits are called *mizu-gashi* (*mizu* means water and *gashi* means sweets), and they have been eaten as a snack or dessert according to availability since olden times. So *mizu-gashi*, which are natural products containing fruit sugar, may be the healthiest and most international dessert. The truth is that adequate amounts of sugar are good not only for our bodies, but also for our minds.

Menu planning (*Kon-date*)

Most Japanese people plan menus for each meal, especially for dinner. They call it 'making kon-date'. The purpose of making 'kon-date' is to plan a well-balanced menu, making sure to include a wide variety of foods in each meal. They consider the nutritional value, taste, flavoring, texture, temperature, and how the combination of dishes will complement one other.

In Japan, it is generally said that people should eat 14 different kinds of food daily, not including seasonings, salt and drinks – cereals such as rice and wheat, potatoes, sugar, soy products, nuts, vegetables, fruit, mushrooms, seaweed, fish, meat, egg, milk or dairy products and oil. When planning your menu, try to combine as many of these foods as possible. Of course, it is very difficult to prepare all 14 kinds of these foods every day, especially seaweed and soy products, which are Japanese favorites. But use as many ingredients as possible on a daily basis. Eating small portions of a variety of food automatically prevents overeating and also stimulates the stomach and brain, which is essential to good health.

People may wonder what the recommended daily amount of sugar is. Sugar is often used in the cooking stage of many Japanese dishes and a lot of sugar is contained in snacks, which are eaten at morning and afternoon tea. So if a person eats sweets in moderation, it should not be necessary to worry about sugar intake, but too much sugar should be discouraged. Enjoying a few biscuits, a little chocolate or a piece of cake at tea time may be acceptable, unless you are a child or a manual worker when a little more may be suitable.

Purchase seasonal and fresh food as often as possible and consume it while it is still fresh, because freshly harvested, seasonal food is the most nutritiously valuable. Food gradually loses its nutritional value as it ages after harvesting. Eating seasonal food helps us to realize that we depend on nature's bounty to live.

Breakfast and lunch are important meals as they provide the body with the immediate energy needed to work well. Even if you are on a diet, missing either of these meals is not recommended. Dinner is another meal essential for providing energy for the next day. If you eat only enough to make you feel 70 to 80% full and stop eating three hours before going to bed, this amount will be enough to keep you healthy. It will be gentle on your stomach and deposit less fat in your body.

The 'kon-date', shown in the following pages, are just examples using the recipes in this book. You can also try to make 'kon-date' with your favorite food. For example soup made from any type of vegetables, roast beef with gravy and mashed potatoes, fresh salad, bread and fruit would be a good dinner menu. The important thing is not to prepare particular foods, but to plan a well-balanced diet using a wide variety of food.

Examples of *'kon-date'*

Green tea

Japanese salad

Miso-flavored mackerel

Pork and vegetable soup

Plain rice

Carrot and Potato kimpira

Green beans dressed with ginger and soy

Teriyaki Chicken

Clam soup

Plain rice

Measurements

Measurements differ according to the country. In this book American measurements are used and the international measurements (grams, milliliters, centimeters and degrees of Celsius) are shown in parentheses. Sweetness and saltiness can be different depending on the sugar, the salt and the seasonings used. Results can be influenced also by the taste of the original ingredients. These can vary depending on the variety used, where they have been grown and, in the case of meat, on the type of food on which the animal has been fed. So at first cook by following the recipes and later, if you feel that something needs changing, modify the quantities indicated. Following the recipe at first and then being more adventurous later and thinking flexibly may be the key to finding true enjoyment in your cooking.

Temperature

Fahrenheit = Centigrade x 9/5 +32

Centigrade = (Fahrenheit - 32) x 5/9

Liquid measure

1 teaspoon	5ml
1 tablespoon	15ml
1 cup	240ml

Weight

(1 ounce = grams x 0.035, 1 gram = ounce x 28.35)

1/6 oz	5g
1/3 oz	10g
1/2 oz	15g
1 oz	30g
1 3/4 oz	50g
2 oz	60g
2 1/2 oz	70g
2 4/5 oz	80g
3 1/2 oz	100g
4 oz	115g
5 1/4 oz	150g
7 oz	200g
8 oz	225g
10 1/2 oz	300g
14 oz	400g
16 oz	450g
18 oz	500g
20 oz	570g
24 1/2 oz	700g
31 1/2 oz	900g
35 oz	1kg

Acknowledgments

The recipes in this book were written little by little over several years and finally completed into one book. In order to make every recipe easy, convenient and as delicious as possible, I attempted many different ingredients and flavorings before coming up with the final dish. I especially want to thank my husband and two daughters for always being so supportive with their love and for being the best samplers.

The part I struggled with in creating this book was with the English syntax. Due to my lack of fluency in English, I especially needed to rely on my lovely friends Masahiko and Cheryl Okubo to correct my English and translate some parts. I appreciate them from the bottom of my heart for undertaking this troublesome work and encouraging me throughout the years. Moreover, I am thankful to my friend Ann Wrigglesworth for her kind English review.

In addition, I would like to express my gratitude to the photographer Sadamu Saito and his wife and assistant Takako Saito for their efforts to create beautiful photos. I am also grateful to the designer Hisanori Niizuma, the publishing consultant Koji Chikatani and Emi Nakahara of Tran Net KK,  and the editors of Veronica Lane Books for dealing with my complicated demands and working hard to make this book so wonderful.

Finally, I feel thankful to all of the people from Japan and abroad who gave me opportunities and hints to think about healthy food and eventually led to the completion of this recipe book.

About the Author

Reiko Suenaga

With a PhD in agriculture acquired from Hokkaido University, Ms. Suenaga carried out research on plant biotechnology during her tenure at the Plantech Research Institute of Mitsubishi Chemical Corporation. Her abiding interest in food led her to establish herself as a counselor on food education in 2006.

Her exposure to home cooked meals of various countries while being stationed abroad served as an opportunity for her to see Japanese cuisine in a new light. At present, she offers lessons in Japanese home cooking once a month for non-Japanese residents at her home in Tsukuba city. She resolved to publish this book when she became convinced that there was much wisdom in Japanese food culture that could be applied to help people beset with problems such as obesity and diseases which may be rooted in dietary lifestyles.

Index